Writing Philosophy

A Student's Guide to Writing Philosophy Essays

Lewis Vaughn

New York   Oxford
OXFORD UNIVERSITY PRESS
2006

Oxford University Press, Inc., publishes works that further Oxford University's objective of excellence in research, scholarship, and education.

Oxford   New York
Auckland   Cape Town   Dar es Salaam   Hong Kong   Karachi
Kuala Lumpur   Madrid   Melbourne   Mexico City   Nairobi
New Delhi   Shanghai   Taipei   Toronto

With offices in
Argentina   Austria   Brazil   Chile   Czech Republic   France   Greece
Guatemala   Hungary   Italy   Japan   Poland   Portugal   Singapore
South Korea   Switzerland   Thailand   Turkey   Ukraine   Vietnam

Published by Oxford University Press, Inc.
198 Madison Avenue, New York, New York 10016
http://www.oup.com

Oxford is a registered trademark of Oxford University Press

Library of Congress Cataloging-in-Publication Data

Vaughn, Lewis.
  Writing philosophy : a student's guide to writing philosophy essays / by Lewis Vaughn.
    p. cm.
  Includes index.
  ISBN-10: 0-19-517956-0
  ISBN-13: 978-0-19-517956-9
    1. Philosophy—Authorship.   I. Title.

B52.7.V38 2005
808'.0661—dc22   2005047713

Printing number: 17 16 15 14 13 12 11 10

Printed in the United States of America
on acid-free paper

⊰ Contents ⊱

⇥ Preface ⇤

This text aspires to help philosophy teachers address a big problem—
the conflict between trying to teach course content and dealing with
students who are ill prepared to write papers on that content. The
dilemma is acute because writing is both a valuable teaching tool and
a vehicle for assessing understanding. Using class time to explain the
unique demands of philosophical writing, however, can divert time
and attention from the real meat of a course. (Grading a batch of
poorly written papers, of course, is no fun either.) No book by itself
can teach good writing, just as no book can be a substitute for the
teacher. *Writing Philosophy*, nevertheless, tries to come as close as
possible to the ideal of a brief, self-guided manual that covers the
basics of argumentative essay writing and encourages rapid learning
with minimal teacher input.

This kind of assault on the "writing problem" requires that the
text be maximally self-sufficient, that it lack very few components
that instructors might have to supply. It therefore covers fundamental skills in reading philosophy, composing text, outlining papers,
evaluating arguments, citing sources, avoiding plagiarism, detecting
fallacies, and formatting finished papers. Teachers, of course, may
want to add material to these essentials—but they may not have to.

A guiding principle of this text is that simplicity serves inexperienced writers best: It is better to help students master one straightforward way to write a simple but effective paper than to overwhelm
them with five ways to produce an essay bristling with options. Even
with uncomplicated writing assignments in philosophy, beginners
will have plenty to think about. If they can produce one good but
uncomplicated paper, however, they may be more likely to excel
when confronted with larger writing challenges.

MAIN FEATURES

This book's overall approach has several distinctive components:

- *An introductory chapter on reading philosophy.* This text begins where many teachers think that instruction on writing philosophy *should* begin—with reading philosophy. This coverage consists of a general introduction to philosophy, rules for increasing understanding of philosophical texts, and instruction on writing paraphrases and summaries. This chapter is part of the book's quick-start approach: It gets students writing immediately so that, by Chapter 4, they can attempt full-blown papers.

- *Step-by-step instructions on how to write argumentative essays.* Instructions cover the entire essay-writing process, from formulating a thesis to creating an outline to writing a final draft. These are supplemented with model essays, outlines, introductions, and conclusions.

- *A rulebook format that encapsulates core principles of good writing.* Like the classic *Elements of Style*, this text tries to distill the most helpful writing advice into simple rules that the student can easily remember and readily apply—and that the teacher can refer to in providing feedback on student papers. Rules cover essay organization, sentence structure, documentation styles, plagiarism, grammar, and usage. There are, for example, ten rules on style and content, eight rules on effective sentences, four rules (and multiple instructions) on quotations and documentation, and nine rules on proper word choice.

- *A chapter on recognizing, reading, and evaluating arguments.* Rules also cover the analysis of premises and conclusions, deductive and inductive arguments, and common argument patterns.

- *A chapter on recognizing and avoiding logical fallacies.* The emphasis is on fallacies that are likely to show up in student writing—straw man, ad hominem, appeal to ignorance, hasty generalization, genetic fallacy, appeal to popularity, false dilemma, begging the question, and others.

- *Full coverage of plagiarism and proper acknowledgment of sources.* There are instructions here on how to use two standard documentation systems. The information is meant to be detailed enough to allow students to document their papers properly without having to consult other books or websites on citing sources.

- *A reference guide to common writing errors and skills.* Chapters 7 and 8 constitute a reference section covering basic writing mistakes in sentence construction, writing style, and word choice. Inexperienced writers can read this reference guide straight through or refer to it when specific writing questions arise (by either checking the table of contents or using the book's detailed index). More advanced students can use the guide to hone their writing skills or to refresh their memories about writing fundamentals.

- *Guidelines for formatting papers.* An appendix provides instructions and examples to help beginners format their papers using specifications generally used in the humanities.

TEACHING STRATEGIES

Teachers will differ in how they use *Writing Philosophy* depending on how much class time they want to devote to writing instruction. Here are some of the possibilities:

- Assign the reading of Chapters 1–4 right away; devote a small block of class time to lectures or discussions on Chapters 1 and 2 (possible assignments: writing paraphrases and summaries). Devote another small block of class time to writing a thesis-defense essay (the subject of Chapter 4). Assign the remaining chapters (5–8).

- Assign the reading of Chapters 1–6 during the first weeks of the course along with the writing of paraphrases, summaries, outlines, essay introductions, and—finally—complete papers. Devote some class time to answering questions about the material. Recommend the use of the reference guide (Chapters 7–8).

- At the beginning of the course, assign the reading of the entire book. Throughout the course, assign the writing of several essays of increasing difficulty, providing feedback on them with references to relevant parts of the text.

⊰ PART 1 ⊱

READING AND WRITING

⊰ 1 ⊱

How to Read Philosophy

To write philosophy, you must be able to read philosophy. To read philosophy—to *really* read it with understanding and appreciation—you must cast off the misconceptions that make philosophy seem barren or impenetrable or trifling. You must abandon the myths about philosophy that make it seem like a dark and distant island, way out of the normal shipping lanes and hardly worth an hour's sailing.

You must also be willing to give philosophy a chance, to try to see what countless people have seen in philosophy through the ages. Philosophical ideas have changed the world, altering the lives of innumerable people (not just those of philosophers), inspiring cultures, and driving history. You must try to understand what all the fuss is about.

Philosophers—those who know philosophy best—would tell you that the study of philosophy is well worth the trouble. But you should not take their word for it. You should try to explore the conceptual terrain for yourself. This chapter is designed to help you get started.

WHAT IS PHILOSOPHY?

Whatever else philosophy may be, it is a discipline, a field of inquiry. It is concerned with the examination of beliefs of the most fundamental kind—beliefs that structure our lives, shape our worldviews, and underpin all academic disciplines. A physiologist may want to know how our brains work, but a philosopher asks a deeper question—whether the brain is the same thing as the mind. A lawyer may study how the death penalty is administered in Texas, but a philosopher asks if capital punishment is ever morally permissible. A medical scientist may want to know how a human fetus develops, but a philosopher asks what the moral status of the fetus is. An astrophysicist may study the Big Bang, the cataclysmic explosion thought to have brought the universe into being. But a philosopher asks whether the Big Bang shows that God caused the universe to exist. Someone may wonder if lying to protect a friend is right or wrong, but a philosopher asks *what makes* an action right or wrong. You may find yourself reflecting on the horrific evils of war and famine, but a philosopher asks if these evils can be squared with the existence of an all-powerful, all-knowing, and all-good God.

These points give the lie to a common myth about philosophy— the notion that philosophy is a trivial endeavor, a pretentious exercise in small matters that have no bearing on issues in real life. Obviously, if philosophy is concerned with questions like those just listed, it is about very important issues indeed. Philosophy is frequently concerned with very difficult questions. But difficult questions are not the same thing as trifling questions, and seriously trying to answer the questions does not make you pretentious.

Notice that philosophy is not primarily concerned with what *causes* you to have the particular beliefs you do. It focuses on *whether a belief is worth believing*. Strong emotions, peer pressure, and cultural influences may cause you to adopt certain opinions. But the important question that philosophy would address is whether those opinions are worthy of belief. A belief is worth believing, or accepting, if there are *good reasons* to accept it (see Chapter 2). The better the reasons for acceptance, the more likely the belief is to be true. Philosophy is a critical and wide-ranging search for understanding, and as such it is perfectly suited for this kind of deeper assessment of beliefs.

Sometimes people use the word *philosophy* in a narrower sense, as in "I have a different philosophy of life." Here, philosophy means *worldview*. A worldview is a set of fundamental ideas that help us make sense of a wide range of important issues in life. A worldview defines for us what exists, what should be, and what we can know.

An interesting fact about worldviews is that we all have one. We all have certain ideas about what exists and what doesn't, what kinds of actions are right or wrong, and what type of claims we can know or not know. Even the rejection of all worldviews is a worldview. A vital question, then, is not whether we have a worldview, but whether our worldview is worth having—whether the beliefs that constitute our worldview are true. Since our lives are guided by our philosophy, our worldview had better be good. Using philosophy in the broad sense is the best way we have of evaluating a philosophy in the narrower sense.

We are born into this world at a particular place and time, steeped in the ideas and values of a particular culture, handed ready-made beliefs that may or may not be true and that we may never think to question. Philosophy helps us rise above this predicament, to transcend the narrow and obstructed standpoint from which we may view everything. It helps us examine our unexamined beliefs in the light of reason, look beyond the prejudices that blind us, and see what's real and true. By using the methods of philosophy, we may learn that some of our beliefs are on solid ground and some are not. In either case, through philosophy, our beliefs become truly and authentically ours, and we are more fully in control of the course we take in life.

As you can see, philosophy as a discipline is both broad and deep—but it is not static. More than anything else, philosophy is a *process*, a careful, systematic investigation of fundamental beliefs. When we get involved in the process, we are "doing philosophy." We are doing what both great philosophers and ordinary people have done for thousands of years. To put it more precisely, doing philosophy consists mainly of the systematic use of critical reasoning to explore answers to basic questions, to clarify the meaning of concepts, and to formulate or evaluate logical arguments.

Clarifying the meaning of concepts is important because we cannot evaluate the worth of a belief or statement until we understand what it means. Very often we may think that we understand a concept—until we look more closely at it. Philosophy gives us the tools to take this closer look. The larger and more characteristic part of doing philosophy, however, is the assessment of arguments. As you will see in Chapter 2, in philosophy the term *argument* does not refer to heated disagreements or emotional squabbles. In philosophy, an argument is a statement, or claim, coupled with other statements that are meant to support that statement. The statement being supported is the conclusion, and the statements supporting the conclusion are the premises. The premises are meant to provide reasons for believing that the conclusion is true. A good argument gives us good reasons for accepting a conclusion; a bad argument fails to provide good reasons.

The Divisions of Philosophy

The field of philosophy is concerned with trying to answer some of the toughest and most fundamental questions that can be devised. In a broad sense, philosophy's sphere of interest is literally everything there is. Philosophy divides its subject matter into four main divisions, each of which is a branch of inquiry in its own right with many subcategories. Here's a brief rundown of these divisions and a sampling of the kinds of questions that each asks.

- *Metaphysics* is the study of reality, an inquiry into the fundamental nature of the universe and the things in it. Although it must take into account the findings of science, metaphysics generally focuses on fundamental questions that science cannot address. *Questions of interest:* Is mind the same thing as body? Do people have free will? Is there a God? What is the nature of causality? Is science objective?

- *Axiology* is the study of value, including both aesthetic value and moral value. The study of moral value is known as *ethics*. The study of ethics involves inquiries into the nature of moral judgments, virtues, obligations, and theories. *Questions of interest:* What makes an action right (or wrong)? What moral principles should guide our actions and choices? What things are intrinsically good? Is killing ever morally permissible? Are moral standards objective or subjective?

- *Epistemology* is the study of knowledge. *Questions of interest:* What is knowledge? Does knowledge require certainty? When are we justified in saying that we know something? Is experience a source of knowledge?

- *Logic* is the study of correct reasoning. *Questions of interest:* What are the rules for drawing correct inferences? What is the nature and structure of deductive arguments? How can propositional or predicate logic be used to evaluate arguments? Upon what logical principles does reasoning depend?

In philosophy—and in any other kind of rational inquiry—accepting a conclusion (statement) without good reasons is an elementary mistake in reasoning. Believing a statement without good reasons is a recipe for error; believing a statement for good reasons increases your chances of uncovering the truth. Arguments are therefore a driving force behind the advancement of knowledge in all fields.

When we do philosophy, then, we are likely at some point to be grappling with arguments—we are trying either (1) to devise an argument to support a statement or (2) to evaluate an argument to see if there really are good reasons for accepting its conclusion. Some of this process, of course, gets done in serious discussions with others or in the solitary thoughts of those trying to search for answers to tough philosophical questions. But a great deal of philosophy gets done on paper, where writers try to create or assess arguments in essays or articles or other kinds of text. The purpose of this book is to help you learn how to handle this task—and perhaps even to excel at it.

Trying to write good philosophy papers has consequences. First, writing philosophy can lead to some interesting discoveries, some unsettling and some splendid. Through the process of devising and evaluating arguments, you may come to see that a cherished belief is unsupportable, or that the arguments of others are faulty, or that arguments that you thought were dubious are actually solid. You may even achieve some remarkable insights into an issue that you always found puzzling. Probably for most people, writing philosophy is the best way to think about philosophy. Second, you may become a better thinker. Philosophical thinking is systematic, analytic, productive thinking—which is something you can use in many everyday situations and fields of study. Third, you may come to better understand and appreciate some of the important ideas of the great thinkers of the past. Grasping the significance of such powerful ideas can be deeply satisfying, even liberating. Great ideas have a way of lifting people up from their customary perspective on the world, from which vantage point they can see farther than they thought possible.

READING PHILOSOPHY

In some ways, reading philosophy is like reading the literature of many other fields. It requires a good deal of abstract thought, often involves difficult concepts or extraordinary propositions, and can be intimidating to those who approach the subject for the first time. But in other ways, reading philosophy is fairly distinctive. When you read a philosophical essay, you are not simply trying to glean some facts from it as you might if you were reading a science text or technical report. Neither are you following a story line as if you were reading a mystery novel (although philosophy papers sometimes contain their share of mysteries). In most cases, you are tracing the steps in an argument, trying to see what conclusion the writer wants to prove and whether he or she succeeds in proving it. Along the way, you may encounter several premises with their accompanying analyses, clarifications, explanations, and examples. You may even run into a whole chain of arguments. In the end, if you have read well and the writer has written well, you are left not with a new set of data or a story ending, but with a realization—maybe even a revelation—that a conclusion is, or is not, worthy of belief.

The best way to learn how to read philosophy well is to read philosophy often. You will probably get plenty of chances to do that in your current philosophy course. Having a few rules to guide you in your reading, however, may help shorten the learning curve. As you read, keep the following in mind.

Rule 1-1   Approach the Text with an Open Mind

If you are studying philosophy for the first time, you are likely—at least at first—to find a good bit of the material difficult, strange, or exasperating, sometimes all three at once. That's normal. Philosophy is an exploration of the rugged frontiers of our knowledge of fundamental things, so much of this new territory is likely to seem daunting or unfamiliar. There's also an excellent chance that your first visits to this terrain will be vexing, perhaps even infuriating, because you may sometimes disagree with what you read.

There is no shame in experiencing any of these reactions. They come with the territory. But if you are to make any headway in philosophy and write good papers, you need to try your best to counteract these attitudes and feelings. Remember, philosophy at its best is a fair-minded, fearless search for truth. Anything that interferes with this noble quest must be overcome and cast aside. Here is some advice on how to do that:

- Avoid making a judgment about an essay's ideas or arguments until you fully understand them and have fairly considered them. Make sure you are not reading with the intent to prove the conclusions false (or true). Be open to the possibility that the essay could give you good reasons to change your mind about something.

- Try to maintain a neutral attitude toward the writer, presuming that he or she is neither right nor wrong, neither sinner nor saint. Don't assume that everything a renowned philosopher says must be true, and don't presuppose that everything a philosopher you dislike says must be false. Give the writer the same attention and respect that you would give a friend who is discussing a serious issue with you.

- If you are reading the work of a famous philosopher and you find yourself thinking that his or her ideas are obviously silly or ridiculous, think again. The odds are good that you are misunderstanding what you read. It is wiser to assume that the text offers something of value (even if you disagree with it) and that you need to read more carefully.

- Once you do make a judgment about the value of a writer's ideas, ask yourself what reasons you have to support that judgment. If you cannot think of any reasons, your judgment is suspect. Reconsider your evaluation.

Rule 1-2   Read Actively and Critically

Philosophical reading is intense. It cannot be rushed. It cannot be crammed. It cannot be done while your mind is on automatic pilot. To repeat: When you read philosophy, you are usually trying to follow the twists and turns of an argument (or several arguments), from premises to conclusion, often through side trips to analyses, illustrations, explanations, digressions, and speculations. You want ultimately to arrive at an understanding and appreciation of the writer's work. You want to end up knowing what the writer is trying to prove and whether he or she has proved it. Going this route requires concentration and perseverance.

Philosophical reading is active reading. Instead of reading just to get through a piece of writing, you must take your time and ask yourself what key terms and passages mean, how the argument is structured, what the central thesis is, where the premises are, how certain key ideas are related, whether the main conclusion conflicts with propositions you know are true, even how the material compares with other philosophical writing on the same subject.

Philosophical reading is also critical reading. In critical reading, you ask not what something means but whether a statement is true and if the reasoning is solid. You ask if the conclusion really follows from the premises, whether the premises are true, if the analysis of a term really makes sense, if an argument has been overlooked, if an analogy is weak, whether there are counterexamples to key claims, and whether the claims agree with other things you have good reason to believe.

When you read fiction, you must often "suspend your disbelief" for the sake of the story. That is, to better enjoy the story, you must try to discard any doubts you might have about the realism of the narrative and pretend that the story could actually happen. But when you read philosophy, you must never suspend your disbelief in this way. The whole point of the exercise is to discover whether various claims are worthy of acceptance.

Reading philosophy actively and critically takes time—a lot of time. You simply cannot do it at a fast pace; you have to read slowly and deliberately (and probably do a lot of note-taking and highlighting). Speed-reading is out of the question. Skimming is pointless. Even if you read at a snail's pace, you will probably need to reread the material, perhaps several times. You need to read and reread as many times as necessary to understand the text fully.

Rule 1-3 Identify the Conclusion First, Then the Premises

When you first begin reading philosophical texts, they may seem to you like dark thickets of propositions into which you may not enter without losing your way. But your situation is really not that bad. As we have seen, in argumentative writing (the kind you are most likely to encounter in philosophy), you can depend on there being, well, an argument, a conclusion backed by premises. There could, of course, be several arguments that support the main argument, and the arguments could be complex, but these sets of conclusion-plus-premises will all serve as recognizable guideposts. If you want to penetrate the thicket, then, you must first identify the argument (or arguments). And the key to doing that is to *find the conclusion first, then look for the premises.* (Chapter 2 details how to identify arguments of all kinds, even when they are ensconced among a great deal of nonargumentative prose.)

When you find the main conclusion, you thereby identify the main point of the essay, and you then have the most important clue to the function of all the rest of the text. Once you uncover the point that the writer is trying to prove, finding the supporting premises becomes much easier. And when you isolate the premises, locating the text that explains and amplifies the premises gets easier too. Therefore, the first—and most important—question you can ask about a philosophical essay is, "What claim is the writer trying to prove?"

Rule 1-4 Outline, Paraphrase, or Summarize the Argument

Understanding an essay's argument is so important that testing whether you really "get it" is crucial. You can test your grasp of the argument by outlining, paraphrasing, or summarizing it. If you can lay out an argument's premises and conclusion in an outline, or if you can accurately paraphrase or summarize the argument, you probably have a pretty good understanding of it. Very often students who think they comprehend an argument are surprised to see that they cannot devise an adequate outline or summary of it. Such failures suggest that, although outlining, paraphrasing, or summarizing may seem to some to be unnecessary, it is not—at least not to those new to philosophy.

Outlining an argument means identifying the premises and the conclusion and arranging them in an outline pattern that reveals their relationships. Each of these components should be stated in a complete sentence. In such a pattern, each premise is listed in order on a single line followed by the last line, the conclusion. Like this:

Premise 1

Premise 2

Premise 3

Conclusion

If the premises themselves are supported by arguments (in which the premises are the conclusions), the outline may look like this:

Main premise 1

    supporting premise a

    supporting premise b

Main premise 2

    supporting premise a

    supporting premise b

    supporting premise c

Main premise 3

Conclusion

You may state each of these points in the same language used in the essay or in your own words. Remember, this kind of outline is not a sketch of the entire essay, just of the argument itself. (An outline of the whole essay may include other points besides the parts of the argument.) Very often, however, the outline of the argument will be virtually identical to an outline of the entire essay. In any case, other parts of the essay (for example, introductory background information or extended concluding remarks) will make sense to you only if you fully understand the argument.

To some students, writing a paraphrase or summary of the argument is more helpful than creating an outline. In a paraphrase, you create your own accurate facsimile of the argument, rephrasing it in your own words and expressions. In a summary, you paraphrase *and* condense, distilling the argument into fewer words than the original has. By successfully paraphrasing or summarizing, you demonstrate that you do indeed understand the argument. (See the next section, "Writing a Paraphrase or Summary," for more guidance in these skills.)

Five Common Mistakes in Reading Philosophy

1. Reading philosophy the same way you would read a technical report or a novel.

2. Prejudging the text's argument or author.

3. Failing to *evaluate* what you read.

4. Trying to speed-read or skim.

5. Not reading actively and critically.

Rule 1-5   Evaluate the Argument and Formulate a Tentative Judgment

When you read philosophy, understanding it is just the first step. You also must do something that many beginners find both difficult and alien: You must make an informed judgment about what you read. Simply reiterating what the writer has said will not do. *Your* judgment is what matters here. Mainly, this judgment is your evaluation of the argument presented by the writer—an assessment of

(1) whether the conclusion follows from the premises and (2) whether the premises are true. Only when the answer is *yes* to both these questions can you say that the conclusion of the argument is worthy of acceptance. This kind of evaluation is precisely what your instructor expects when he or she asks you to critique an argumentative essay in philosophy.

A philosophical text, of course, contains more than just a bare-bones argument. Often a considerable amount of space is devoted to explaining the background or history of the topic being addressed, elaborating on each of the premises, discussing the implications of the argument's conclusion, and answering possible criticisms of the essay's main points. Certainly you must take these into account when you are reading and evaluating a philosophical text. But your primary task is to arrive at an honest and well-reasoned assessment of the text's central claim.

WRITING A PARAPHRASE OR SUMMARY

There are three reasons why you should try to master paraphrasing or summarizing an essay's argument. The first one you already know: Paraphrasing or summarizing increases your understanding. The second one is that you need these skills to do well on essay exams, which often ask you to paraphrase or summarize a philosopher's work. The third is that in just about every philosophy paper you write, you will have to restate or condense arguments. Paraphrasing and summarizing are required.

In good essays, writers often paraphrase or summarize an author because their own wording is clearer than that of the original source. They sometimes summarize a passage because the author's original is too long to quote verbatim yet all its main points are worth mentioning. Whether they add a paraphrase or summary, however, they are careful to cue the reader about it. Just as quotations should be introduced properly and explained in a paper, so must paraphrases and summaries. Readers should never have to guess whose ideas are being put forth, what a paraphrase or summary means, or how it relates to the rest of the paper.

The first step in paraphrasing or summarizing is understanding the text. Do not begin writing until you have read the essay and think that you understand it well. In other words, do not try to paraphrase or summarize until you have followed Rule 1-2: Read actively and critically.

Paraphrasing is a matter of rewriting text—accurately representing the text's meaning but doing so in *your* words, not in a barely disguised rendition of the author's words. A paraphrase is not a condensation, so in most cases any paraphrase you produce should contain close to the same number of words as the author's original.

In paraphrasing, you try to capture the gist of passages—perhaps just the paragraph that contains the argument in a nutshell, or the section of the paper that discusses a major point, or even the entire essay, point by point. If you want in-depth understanding of what a philosopher is saying, there is no better way than to paraphrase the entire essay.

Consider this passage taken from the essay in the next section; read the paraphrase of it that follows.

PASSAGE

To make the point clearer, consider a different matter. In some societies, people believe the earth is flat. In other societies, such as our own, people believe that the earth is (roughly) spherical. Does it follow, from the mere fact that people disagree, that there is no "objective truth" in geography? Of course not; we would never draw such a conclusion because we realize that, in their beliefs about the world, the members of some societies might simply be wrong. There is no reason to think that if the world is round everyone must know it. Similarly, there is no reason to think that if there is moral truth everyone must know it. The fundamental mistake in the Cultural Differences Argument [which says that because societies disagree on morality there must be no objective morality] is that it attempts to derive a substantive conclusion about a subject from the mere fact that people disagree about it.[1]

PARAPHRASE I

Rachels tries to show that disagreement among societies about moral values does not, in itself, show that there is no such thing as objective morality. In some societies, people believe that the earth is flat. In our own society, we believe that the earth is spherical. This case of clashing views, however, does not show that there are no objective truths about geography. It is possible that such disagreements happen because some people have false beliefs. Why should we think that if the world is round

[1]Excerpted from chapter 2 of James Rachels, *The Elements of Moral Philosophy* (New York: McGraw-Hill Higher Education, 2003), 20–21.

everyone must realize it? Likewise, if there is such a thing as objective moral truths, we have no evidence to think that everyone would know these truths. We must conclude that the mistake in the cultural difference argument is thinking that we can draw a conclusion about something from the mere fact that people disagree about it.

This paraphrase is *not* acceptable. It is fairly accurate, but it mimics the words and phrases of the original too closely. It repeats, for example, some parts word for word: "people believe that the earth is flat," "believe that the earth is . . . spherical," "if the world is round, everyone must," and "from the mere fact that people disagree about it." Also, some sentences that are not verbatim are obviously and blatantly modeled after Rachels's. The close mimicry of this passage is a problem for two reasons. First, it diminishes the opportunities for better understanding of the text because it is mere repetition instead of thoughtful, thorough recasting. Second, the paraphrase constitutes plagiarism. It repeats many of Rachels's words verbatim without enclosing them in quotation marks, and it closely apes his ideas and sentence patterns without acknowledging Rachel as the source. (See Rules 6-2 and 6-3.)

Here is a better paraphrase:

PARAPHRASE 2

Rachels shows that the cultural differences argument is unfounded and is, in fact, based on a mistake. He argues that we cannot infer that objective morality does not exist from the fact that societies have conflicting views about moral judgments. To make his case, he uses an example from an unrelated field, geography. Some societies think the earth flat; some, spherical. What can we conclude from such a disagreement? It surely would be illogical to conclude that because people differ on geographical facts there must be no objective geological facts. After all, Rachels says, people in different societies "might simply be wrong." Likewise, moral disagreements may simply indicate that some people are mistaken and some are not. Therefore, there is no good reason to accept the cultural difference argument.[44]

This paraphrase is accurate and does not improperly borrow Rachels's words or sentence patterns. It includes a citation and clear indications of which ideas have been derived from Rachels.

A summary must accurately capture a text's main ideas in just a few words. You should be able to summarize the main points of an entire essay (that is, the premises and conclusion) in less than 150 words. Those words, of course, must be your own.

Look at this longer excerpt from the same essay:

Cultural Relativism is a theory about the nature of morality. At first blush it seems quite plausible. However, like all such theories, it may be evaluated by subjecting it to rational analysis; and when we analyze Cultural Relativism, we find that it is not so plausible as it first appears to be.

The first thing we need to notice is that at the heart of Cultural Relativism there is a certain *form of argument*. The strategy used by cultural relativists is to argue from facts about the differences between cultural outlooks to a conclusion about the status of morality. Thus we are invited to accept this reasoning:

1. The Greeks believed it was wrong to eat the dead, whereas the Callatians believed it was right to eat the dead.

2. Therefore, eating the dead is neither objectively right nor objectively wrong. It is merely a matter of opinion that varies from culture to culture.

A proper summary of this passage should accurately encapsulate its main points, like this:

Rachels says that the moral theory known as cultural relativism may appear credible initially, but it cannot withstand critical assessment. The main argument for the theory says that since moral outlooks vary from culture to culture, there is no objective moral standard by which everyone can be judged. There is only a world of moral beliefs that vary from one society to the next.[44]

Again, Rachels is clearly credited, and the source is documented.

APPLYING THE RULES

Let's apply the preceding rules to Rachels's entire essay.[2] Read it and study the comments that follow.

Cultural Relativism
James Rachels

1. Cultural Relativism, as it has been called, challenges our ordinary belief in the objectivity and universality of moral truth. It says, in effect,

---

[2]Excerpted from James Rachels, *The Elements of Moral Philosophy*, McGraw-Hill Higher Education, 2003. Reproduced with permission of The McGraw-Hill Companies.

that there is no such thing as universal truth in ethics; there are only the various cultural codes, and nothing more. Moreover, our own code has no special status; it is merely one among many. . . .

2. Cultural Relativism is a theory about the nature of morality. At first blush it seems quite plausible. However, like all such theories, it may be evaluated by subjecting it to rational analysis; and when we analyze Cultural Relativism, we find that it is not so plausible as it first appears to be.

3. The first thing we need to notice is that at the heart of Cultural Relativism there is a certain *form of argument*. The strategy used by cultural relativists is to argue from facts about the differences between cultural outlooks to a conclusion about the status of morality. Thus we are invited to accept this reasoning:

4. (1) The Greeks believed it was wrong to eat the dead, whereas the Callatians believed it was right to eat the dead.

   (2) Therefore, eating the dead is neither objectively right nor objectively wrong. It is merely a matter of opinion that varies from culture to culture.

5. Or, alternatively:

6. (1) The Eskimos see nothing wrong with infanticide, whereas Americans believe infanticide is immoral.

   (2) Therefore, infanticide is neither objectively right nor objectively wrong. It is merely a matter of opinion, which varies from culture to culture.

7. Clearly, these arguments are variations of one fundamental idea. They are both special cases of a more general argument, which says:

8. (1) Different cultures have different moral codes.

   (2) Therefore, there is no objective "truth" in morality. Right and wrong are only matters of opinion, and opinions vary from culture to culture.

9. We may call this the Cultural Differences Argument. To many people, it is persuasive. But from a logical point of view, is it sound?

10. It is not sound. The trouble is that the conclusion does not follow from the premise—that is, even if the premise is true, the conclusion still might be false. The premise concerns what people *believe*—in some societies, people believe one thing; in other societies, people believe differently. The conclusion, however, concerns what *really is the case*. The trouble is that this sort of conclusion does not follow logically from this sort of premise.

11. Consider again the example of the Greeks and Callatians. The Greeks believed it was wrong to eat the dead; the Callatians believed it was right. Does it follow, from the mere fact that they disagreed, that there is no objective truth in the matter? No, it does not follow; for it could be that the practice was objectively right (or wrong) and that one or the other of them was simply mistaken.

12. To make the point clearer, consider a different matter. In some societies, people believe the earth is flat. In other societies, such as our own, people believe that the earth is (roughly) spherical. Does it follow, from the mere fact that people disagree, that there is no "objective truth" in geography? Of course not; we would never draw such a conclusion because we realize that, in their beliefs about the world, the members of some societies might simply be wrong. There is no reason to think that if the world is round everyone must know it. Similarly, there is no reason to think that if there is moral truth everyone must know it. The fundamental mistake in the Cultural Differences Argument is that it attempts to derive a substantive conclusion about a subject from the mere fact that people disagree about it.

13. This is a simple point of logic, and it is important not to misunderstand it. We are not saying (not yet, anyway) that the conclusion of the argument is false. That is still an open question. The logical point is just that the conclusion does not *follow from* the premise. This is important, because in order to determine whether the conclusion is true, we need arguments in its support. Cultural Relativism proposes this argument, but unfortunately the argument turns out to be fallacious. So it proves nothing.

What might be the result of your conscientiously following the rules as you read this selection? Here is a brief demonstration:

Rule 1-1. This little essay is particularly well suited to testing students' ability to approach a piece of philosophical writing with an open mind. The essay's topic is the common argument for cultural relativism that the author calls the "cultural differences argument." Cultural relativism is the view that there is no such thing as objective morality but that morality is relative to one's culture. To put it another way, what makes an action right is that one's culture approves of it. The cultural differences argument is a popular argument in favor of cultural relativism—an argument that many (most?) college students assume to be perfectly sound. There is a good chance, therefore, that you would come to this essay strongly predisposed *toward* the argument and *against* any criticisms of it.

To follow Rule 1-1, however, you would need to restrain any tendency to reject the author's argument out of hand. You would try *not* to prejudge the quality of the argument before you have read and understood it. This means being open to the possibility that the cultural differences argument is indeed faulty.

Conversely, you would not want to assume automatically that the author is right. James Rachels is a famous name in philosophy and a well respected one too. This fact should not predetermine the outcome of your evaluation of his argument.

Rules 1-2 and 1-3. Reading the essay actively and critically (and repeatedly) would help you see, among other things, that (1) the thesis statement (the conclusion of the author's argument) is in paragraph 10: "[The cultural differences argument] is not sound"; (2) the first nine paragraphs are not part of the essay's argument but simply introduce the topic and explain the argument to be critiqued; (3) the essay's argument has one explicit premise ("The trouble is that the conclusion does not follow from the premise—that is, even if the premise is true, the conclusion still might be false"), which first appears in paragraph 10 and is elaborated on in paragraphs 11–13; and (4) the author's description of the cultural differences argument seems to be fair and accurate.

Rule 1-4. An outline of the essay's argument would look like this:

PREMISE: The conclusion of the cultural differences argument does not follow from its premise.

CONCLUSION: The cultural differences argument is not sound.

Rule 1-5. As you can see, the essay puts forth a simple argument. Evaluating the argument should be straightforward, especially if you understand the basics of arguments explained in Chapter 2. In your assessment, your main priority would be to determine whether the essay's conclusion follows from the premise and whether the premise is true. The essay's conclusion does indeed follow: From a premise stating that the conclusion of the cultural differences argument does not follow from its premise, we can readily conclude that the cultural differences argument is not sound. Premise 1 is true; from the fact that different cultures have different moral codes, we cannot conclude that there is no such thing as objective truth in morality.

QUICK REVIEW: Reading Philosophy

- Philosophy is not primarily concerned with what causes you to have particular beliefs; it focuses on whether those beliefs are worth having.

- Philosophy helps you evaluate your worldview.

- Through philosophy, your beliefs can become truly and authentically yours, and you can be more fully in control of your life.

- In philosophy, an argument is a statement, or claim, coupled with other statements that are meant to support that statement.

- The productive reading of philosophy requires an open mind, an active and critical approach, and the identification of the conclusion and premises.

- Outlining, paraphrasing, or summarizing can enhance your understanding of a philosophical essay.

How to Read an Argument

To a large extent, to read and write philosophy is to read and write arguments, for logical argument is at the heart of philosophy. When we do philosophy, we are usually either evaluating or constructing arguments. The philosophy that we read will most likely contain arguments, and our understanding of the text will hang on our ability to identify and understand those arguments. Most often the quality of the philosophical essays we write will depend heavily on the quality of the arguments we craft. Learning the fundamentals of logical argument, then, is a prerequisite for making sense out of philosophy and writing good philosophy papers. This chapter will get you going in the right direction by showing you how to pick out arguments from passages of nonargumentative prose, assess the quality of different kinds of arguments, devise good arguments, and recognize defective arguments when you see them.

PREMISES AND CONCLUSIONS

A *statement*, or claim, is an assertion that something is or is not the case. It is the kind of utterance that is *either true or false*. These are statements:

A tree is growing in the quad.

I am shocked and dismayed.

2 + 2 = 4

Time heals all wounds.

The universe is fifteen billion years old.

These, however, are *not* statements:

Why is a tree growing in the quad?

Why are you shocked and dismayed?

Stop being stupid.

Holy cow!

The first two sentences are questions; the third, a command or request; and the fourth, an exclamation. These are not the kind of things that can be true or false.

An *argument* is a combination of statements in which some of them are intended to support another one of them. That is, in an argument, some statements are intended to provide reasons for believing that another statement is true. The statements supposedly providing the support are known as *premises;* the statement being supported is known as the *conclusion.*

A basic task that rational beings engage in is trying to determine how strongly to believe a statement. A fundamental principle in philosophy (and our daily lives) is that the strength of our belief in a statement should depend on the strength of the reasons for believing it. A statement supported by strong reasons is worthy of strong acceptance. A statement supported by weaker reasons deserves weaker acceptance. The analysis of arguments is the primary method we use to discover how much credence to give statements and reasons. This method is essential not only in philosophy but in all fields of knowledge.

By now you probably have guessed that logical arguments are not arguments in the ordinary sense of shouting matches, heated debates, or angry squabbles. In philosophy and other kinds of intellectual exploration, an argument is a conclusion meant to be backed by reasons. Arguments in the ordinary sense are beside the point.

We must also distinguish between logical argument and persuasion. They are *not* synonymous. Presenting an argument is a way to demonstrate that a conclusion (a statement or belief) is warranted, that the conclusion is worthy of acceptance. This demonstration may or may not persuade someone to accept the conclusion; the argument's persuasiveness or lack thereof is a completely separate matter. On the other hand, you may be able to persuade someone to accept a statement through the use of psychological or rhetorical trickery, emotional language, fallacious appeals, threats of force, deceit, and many other ploys. But if you do, you will not have shown that the statement is worthy of belief, for you will not have provided any reasons for accepting it.

Here are some arguments:

ARGUMENT 1

Chivalry is dead. My instructor says so.

ARGUMENT 2

If Michigan wins, there will be a riot in the stadium. They will definitely win. So the riot is a sure thing.

ARGUMENT 3

Ninety-eight percent of the students are conservatives. Joan is a student, so she's probably a conservative too.

ARGUMENT 4

All men are mortal. Socrates is a man. Therefore, Socrates is mortal.

Now let's label the premises and conclusion in each one:

ARGUMENT 1

[CONCLUSION] Chivalry is dead. [PREMISE] My instructor says so.

ARGUMENT 2

[PREMISE] If Michigan wins, there will be a riot in the stadium. [PREMISE] They will definitely win. [CONCLUSION] So the riot is a sure thing.

ARGUMENT 3

[PREMISE] Ninety-eight percent of the students are conservatives. [PREMISE] Joan is a student, [CONCLUSION] so she's probably a conservative too.

ARGUMENT 4

[PREMISE] All men are mortal. [PREMISE] Socrates is a man. [CONCLUSION] Therefore, Socrates is mortal.

Notice that these arguments differ in the placement and number of their parts. In argument 1, the conclusion comes first, then the premise. In the other three arguments, the conclusion comes last.

Argument 1 has one premise, but arguments 2, 3, and 4 have two premises each. The point is that arguments come in all kinds of configurations. An argument could have one premise, or two, or ten, or more. Sometimes a premise (or even the conclusion) is unstated, leaving the reader to fill in the blank (more on uncovering implicit premises later). But regardless of their structure, all arguments must have a conclusion and at least one premise. As long as this requirement is met, arguments can vary all over the map.

Now take a look at this passage:

The stock market has tanked. Brokers are skittish. The Dow is the lowest it's been in ten years. We're pretty scared about all this.

Is there an argument here? If you think so, where is the conclusion? Where are the premises? Alas, this little observation about the stock market is not an argument. The passage consists of a series of statements with no conclusion in sight. There is no statement that other statements are supporting.

It is easy enough, however, to turn these statements into an argument. Look:

ARGUMENT 5

The world of stocks and bonds is in for a rough ride because the stock market has tanked, brokers are skittish, and the Dow is the lowest it's been in ten years.

This passage is now a bone fide argument. The conclusion is "It's clear that the world of stocks and bonds is in for a rough ride." The three statements that follow support the conclusion.

Four Common Mistakes in Evaluating Arguments

1. Failing to distinguish between the logical structure of an argument and the truth of its premises.
2. Thinking that merely stating views is the same thing as presenting an argument.
3. Thinking that persuading someone to accept a claim is the same thing as presenting an argument.
4. Failing to distinguish between arguments and nonargumentative material.

Being able to distinguish arguments from nonargumentative material is a very valuable skill, and the sooner you master it the better. You will often encounter passages that seem to conceal an argument somewhere but do not. Many people (are you one of them?) think that if they clearly and firmly state their beliefs, they have given an argument. Sometimes they fill whole essays with many well-made statements and interesting points, thinking that they are making a strong case—but there is no argument anywhere. Despite all the verbiage, such essays fail to provide the reader with a single good reason to accept any assertion. As we have seen, a collection of unsupported statements does not an argument make. For there to be an argument, at least one statement must provide reasons for accepting another. Now consider this passage:

Johnson is absolutely the worst governor this state has ever had. I don't understand how anyone can read about the governor's exploits in the paper and still support him. Haven't the citizens of this state had enough scandal and corruption in the governor's office? I am aghast at Johnson's outrageous behavior and obvious ineptness.

Has the writer presented an argument? Once again, no. This passage is certainly an expression of displeasure and perhaps even of anger and disgust. But there is no claim supported with reasons. With some major alterations, however, we can turn the passage into an argument:

ARGUMENT 6

Johnson is absolutely the worst governor this state has ever had. He has embezzled money from the state's treasury. He has ruined the state's economy. And he has used his office to persecute those he doesn't like. I am aghast at Johnson's outrageous behavior and obvious ineptness.

If we laid out the argument so we can more clearly see its structure (that is, if we outline it), it would look like this:

PREMISE 1: He has embezzled money from the state's treasury.

PREMISE 2: He has ruined the state's economy.

PREMISE 3: And he has used his office to persecute those he doesn't like.

CONCLUSION: Johnson is absolutely the worst governor this state has ever had.

Notice that the last sentence of the passage is not shown in this argument outline. That's because it is not part of the argument; it is not supporting the conclusion. It is simply an expression of the writer's reaction to the governor's misdeeds.

Logical arguments often come packaged with all sorts of nonargumentative material—introductory remarks, explanations, redundancies, descriptions, asides, examples, and more. The trick is to separate the premises and conclusion from all the other stuff. Once you pinpoint those, spotting the extraneous material is fairly straightforward.

As noted in Rule 1-3, the simplest way to locate an argument is to find its conclusion first, then its premises. Zeroing in on conclusions and premises can be a lot easier if you keep an eye out for *indicator words*. Indicator words often tag along with arguments and indicate that a conclusion or premise may be nearby. Arguments 2–5 have several indicator words. Arguments 2 and 3 contain the word *so*, which points to their respective conclusions. In argument 4 the indicator word *therefore* tells us that the conclusion follows. In argument 5 the indicator word *because* signals the presence of the three premises.

Here are a few conclusion indicator words:

consequently	as a result
thus	hence
therefore	so
it follows that	which means that

Here are some premise indicator words:

in view of the fact	assuming that
because	since
due to the fact that	for
the reason being	given that

Just remember that indicator words do not *guarantee* the presence of conclusions and premises. They are simply telltale signs.

There is one final wrinkle you should understand: Some arguments have unstated, or implicit, premises, and a few even have unstated conclusions. For example:

ARGUMENT 7

Any judge who supports capital punishment for juvenile offenders is an enemy of the Bill of Rights. Judge Simpson is definitely an enemy of the Bill of Rights.

The conclusion of this argument is "Judge Simpson is definitely an enemy of the Bill of Rights," and the only premise is the first statement. But there seems to be a leap of logic from the premise to the conclusion. Something is missing. The conclusion follows logically only if we insert an additional premise to bridge the gap, something like this:

ARGUMENT 7A

Any judge who supports capital punishment for juvenile offenders is an enemy of the Bill of Rights. Judge Simpson supports capital punishment for juvenile offenders. Therefore, Judge Simpson is definitely an enemy of the Bill of Rights.

Now we can see both the stated premise as well as the one left unmentioned, and we can conduct a complete evaluation.

When you're evaluating an argument, you should always bring any implicit premises out into the open. Finding the implicit premise makes evaluation easier. It also helps you avoid falling into a logical trap. Often premises that are left unstated are dubious or false. You should never let questionable premises slide by unnoticed.

JUDGING ARGUMENTS

In Chapter 1, we saw the importance of approaching a philosophical text with an open mind (Rule 1-1); reading actively and critically (Rule 1-2); identifying the conclusion first, then the premises (Rule 1-3); outlining, paraphrasing, or summarizing the argument (Rule 1-4); and evaluating the argument and formulating a tentative judgment (Rule 1-5). Chances are, you are most intimidated by Rule 1-5. You need not be. The following rules elaborate on Rule 1-5 and detail more techniques for systematically sizing up arguments, even complex ones that are buried in a tangle of extraneous material.

Rule 2-1   Know the Basics of Deductive and Inductive Arguments

As we saw in Chapter 1, a good argument gives us good reasons for accepting a conclusion; a bad argument fails to provide good reasons. To tell the difference—and to do so consistently—you need to understand the different forms that arguments can take.

Arguments come in two basic types: *deductive* and *inductive*. Deductive arguments are supposed to offer logically *conclusive* support for their conclusions. If a deductive argument actually manages to provide logically conclusive support for its conclusion, it is said to be *valid*. If it fails to provide logically conclusive support for the conclusion, it is said to be *invalid*. If a deductive argument is valid, it has this peculiar characteristic: If its premises are true, its conclusion absolutely *must be true*. In a valid argument, *it is impossible for the premises to be true and the conclusion false*. Notice that *valid* is not a synonym for *true*. A valid argument is simply one that has the kind of structure, or form, that *guarantees* that if the premises are true, the conclusion is also true. A valid argument, then, is one whose conclusion *follows from the premises*.

Take a look at this simple deductive argument:

ARGUMENT 8

All soldiers are brave.

Roy is a soldier.

Therefore, Roy is brave.

In this argument, you can see that if the premises are true, then the conclusion absolutely must be true. There is no way that the conclusion can be anything else but true. The form of the argument—not its content—is what guarantees this outcome. Notice that the first premise is actually false, but the argument is still valid. We could plug completely different statements into this argument, but as long as the form stays the same, the argument would remain valid.

Consider this deductive argument:

ARGUMENT 9

If stealing harms people, then it is morally wrong.

Stealing does harm people.

Therefore, stealing is morally wrong.

This argument is also valid. If it is true that *if stealing harms people then it is morally wrong*, and if it is also true that *stealing does harm people*, then the conclusion (*stealing is morally wrong*) must be true as well.

Traditionally, philosophers have symbolized the form of deductive arguments by using letters to stand for parts of the argument. The form of argument 9, then, can be symbolized like this:

If p, then q.

p.

Therefore, q.

Here, the letters p and q represent the two statements in the argument. Notice that the first premise is a compound statement, which is made up of two constituent statements p and q. We could insert any statements we want into this valid form, and it would still be the case that if the premises are true, the conclusion must be true.

Unlike deductive arguments, inductive arguments are meant to provide *probable* support for their conclusions. If an inductive argument succeeds in providing such probable support, it is said to be *strong*. In a strong argument, if the premises are true, the conclusion is probably true. If an inductive argument fails to provide probable support for its conclusion, it is said to be *weak*. Like a valid argument, a strong argument is one whose conclusion *follows from the premises*.

So inductive arguments cannot guarantee the truth of their conclusions as deductive arguments can. They can only render their conclusions probable—that is, more likely to be true than not. In inductive arguments, then, it is possible for the premises to be true and the conclusions false.

Consider these two inductive arguments:

ARGUMENT 10

Almost all of the students at this school are Democrats.

Therefore, Maria, who is a student here, is probably a Democrat too.

ARGUMENT 11

Ninety percent of the Republicans I know are Volvo owners.

Therefore, 90 percent of all Republicans are probably Volvo owners.

Argument 10 is strong. If it is true that almost all the students at the school are Democrats, then it is likely that Maria is a Democrat too. Yet it is possible for the premise of argument 10 to be true and the conclusion false.

Argument 11, on the other hand, is weak. Even if 90 percent of the Republicans one person knows own Volvos, it does not follow that *all* Republicans are Volvo owners. The relatively small sample of Republican Volvo owners does not allow us to generalize to millions of Republicans.

We can now be more precise about the characteristics of good arguments. Good arguments (whether deductive or inductive) must be well reasoned—that is, they must be either valid or strong. But good arguments must also have true premises. An argument is not good (does not give us good reasons for accepting a conclusion) unless it is valid or strong *and* all of its premises are true. A valid deductive argument with true premises is said to be *sound*. A strong inductive argument with true premises is said to be *cogent*. So a good deductive argument is sound; a good inductive argument is cogent.

Rule 2-2   Determine Whether the Conclusion Follows from the Premises

Usually, the first step in assessing the worth of an argument is to determine whether the conclusion follows from the premises—that is, whether the argument is valid or strong. If the conclusion does not follow from the premises, then the argument cannot give you good reasons to accept the conclusion. The argument is bad—even if the premises are true.

Very often, when you examine an argument, you will see right away whether the conclusion follows from the premises. At other times, you may have to think about the argument's structure for a while. But in many cases, you will need some help in sizing up the argument—the kind of help offered in the following pages.

Fortunately, deductive arguments often occur in certain classic patterns. The forms, or structures, of the arguments show up again and again. Being familiar with these patterns can help you quickly determine whether an argument is valid.

Consider argument 9:

ARGUMENT 9

If stealing harms people, then it is morally wrong.

Stealing does harm people.

Therefore, stealing is morally wrong.

We symbolized this argument like this:

If *p*, then *q*.

p.

Therefore, *q*.

This kind of argument is known as a *conditional* (also, *hypothetical*). A conditional argument contains at least one conditional, or if-then, premise (If *p*, then *q*). The first half of a conditional premise (the *if* part) is called the *antecedent*. The second half (the *then* part) is known as the *consequent*. It happens that argument 9 is a conditional argument in a classic pattern called *modus ponens* (or *affirming the antecedent*). In *modus ponens*, the second premise affirms the antecedent of the first premise. Any argument using this pattern or form is *always* valid. So if you come across an argument in this pattern, you will know that it is valid—no matter what the statements say.

Another classic conditional pattern is called *modus tollens*, or denying the consequent. Look:

ARGUMENT 12

If the cat is on the mat, then she is asleep.

But she is not asleep.

Therefore, she is not on the mat.

ARGUMENT 13

If the mind is identical to the brain, then damaging the brain will damage the mind.

But damaging the brain will not damage the mind.

Therefore, the mind is not identical to the brain.

Modus tollens, then, is symbolized like this:

If *p*, then *q*.

Not *q*.

Therefore, not *p*.

Any argument having this form is valid.

Here's a slightly more involved conditional form known as *hypothetical syllogism*:

ARGUMENT 14

If the cat is on the mat, then she is asleep.

If she is asleep, then she is dreaming.

Therefore, if the cat is on the mat, then she is dreaming.

The hypothetical syllogism is symbolized like this:

If p, then q.

If q, then r.

Therefore, if p, then r.

Any argument having this form is valid.

QUICK REVIEW: Valid Conditional Argument Forms

AFFIRMING THE ANTECEDENT (MODUS PONENS)	DENYING THE CONSEQUENT (MODUS TOLLENS)
If p, then q.	If p, then q.
p.	Not q.
Therefore, q.	Therefore, not p.

HYPOTHETICAL SYLLOGISM

If p, then q.

If q, then r.

Therefore, if p, then r.

There are also common forms that are *not* valid. This one is known as *denying the antecedent*:

ARGUMENT 15

If the cat is on the mat, then she is asleep.

She is not on the mat.

Therefore, she is not asleep.

Denying the antecedent is symbolized like this:

If p, then q.

Not p.

Therefore, not q.

Finally, there is this invalid form, called *affirming the consequent.*

ARGUMENT 16

If the cat is on the mat, then she is asleep.

She is asleep.

Therefore, she is on the mat.

Affirming the consequent is symbolized like this:

If p, then q.

q.

Therefore, p.

The best way to use these argument forms to evaluate deductive arguments is to memorize them so you can more easily identify examples of the forms when you encounter them. Then you need only match the form of the deductive argument you are evaluating with one of these classic forms. If the argument matches one of the valid forms, it is valid; if one of the invalid forms, it is invalid.

QUICK REVIEW: Invalid Conditional Argument Forms

DENYING THE ANTECEDENT	AFFIRMING THE CONSEQUENT
If p, then q.	If p, then q.
Not p.	q.
Therefore, not q.	Therefore, p.

Inductive arguments also have distinctive forms, and being familiar with the forms can help you evaluate the arguments. Let's look at three common forms of inductive arguments.

In *enumerative induction*, we arrive at a generalization about an entire group of things after observing just some members of the group. Here is a typical enumerative inductive argument:

ARGUMENT 17

Every formatted disk I have bought from the computer store is defective.

Therefore, all formatted disks sold at the computer store are probably defective.

ARGUMENT 18

All the hawks in this wildlife sanctuary that I have observed have had red tails.

Therefore, all the hawks in this sanctuary probably have red tails.

ARGUMENT 19

Sixty percent of the Bostonians I have interviewed in various parts of the city are pro-choice.

Therefore, 60 percent of all Bostonians are probably pro-choice.

As you can see, enumerative induction has this form:

X percent of the observed members of group A have property P.

Therefore, X percent of all members of group A probably have property P.

The observed members of the group are simply a sample of the entire group. So based on what we know about this sample, we can generalize to all the members. But how do we know whether such an argument is strong? Everything depends on the sample. If the sample is large enough and representative enough, we can safely assume that our generalization drawn from the sample is probably an accurate reflection of the whole group of members. A sample is representative of an entire group only if each member of the group has an equal chance of being included in the sample. In general the larger the sample, the greater the probability that it accurately reflects the nature of the group as a whole. Often common sense tells us when a sample is too small.

We do not know how many formatted disks from the computer store are in the sample mentioned in argument 17. But if the number is several dozen and the disks were bought over a period of weeks or months, the sample is probably sufficiently large and representative. If so, the argument is strong. Likewise, in argument 18 we don't know the size of the sample or how it was obtained. But if the sample was taken from all the likely spots in the sanctuary where hawks live, and if several hawks were observed in each location, the sample is probably adequate—and the argument is strong. In argument 19, if the sample consists of a handful of Bostonians interviewed on a few street corners, the sample is definitely inadequate and the argument is weak. But if the sample consists of several hundred people, and if every member of the whole group has an equal chance of being included in the sample, then the sample would be good enough to allow us to accurately generalize about the whole population. Typically, selecting such a sample of a large population is done by professional polling organizations.

In the argument form known as *analogical induction* (or *argument by analogy*), we reason in this fashion: Two or more things are similar in several ways; therefore, they are probably similar in one further way. Consider this argument:

ARGUMENT 20

Humans can walk upright, use simple tools, learn new skills, and devise deductive arguments.

Chimpanzees can walk upright, use simple tools, and learn new skills.

Therefore, chimpanzees can probably devise deductive arguments.

This argument says that because chimpanzees are similar to humans in several respects, they probably are similar to humans in one further respect.

Here's an argument by analogy that has become a classic in philosophy:

ARGUMENT 21

A watch is a complex mechanism with many parts that seem arranged to achieve a specific purpose—a purpose chosen by the watch's designer. In similar fashion, the universe is a complex mechanism with many parts that seem arranged to achieve a specific purpose. Therefore, the universe must also have a designer.

We can represent the form of an argument by analogy in this way:

X has properties P_1, P_2, P_3 plus the property P_4.

Y has properties P_1, P_2, and P_3.

Therefore, Y probably has property P_4.

The strength of an analogical induction depends on the relevant similarities between the two things compared. The more relevant similarities there are, the greater the probability that the conclusion is true. In argument 20, several similarities are noted. But there are some unmentioned dissimilarities. The brain of a chimpanzee is smaller and more primitive than that of a human, a difference that probably inhibits higher intellectual functions such as logical argument. Argument 19, then, is weak. A common response to argument 21 is that the argument is weak because, although the universe resembles a watch in some ways, in other ways it does not resemble a watch. Specifically, the universe also resembles a living thing.

The third type of inductive argument is known as *inference to the best explanation*, a kind of reasoning that we all use daily and that is at the heart of scientific investigations. Recall that an argument gives us reasons for believing *that* something is the case. An *explanation*, on the other hand, states *how* or *why* something is the case. It attempts to clarify or elucidate, not offer proof. For example:

1. Megan definitely understood the material, for she could answer every question on the test.

2. Megan understood the material because she has a good memory.

Sentence 1 is an argument. The conclusion is "Megan definitely understood the material," and the reason (premise) given for believing that the conclusion is true is "for she could answer every question on the test." Sentence 2, however, is an explanation. It does not try to present reasons for believing something; it has nothing to prove. Instead, it tries to show why something is the way it is (why Megan understood the material). Sentence 2 assumes that Megan understood the material and then tries to explain why. Such explanations play a crucial role in inference to the best explanation.

In this type of inductive argument, we begin with premises about a phenomenon or state of affairs to be explained. Then we reason from those premises to an explanation for that state of affairs. We try to produce not just any old explanation but the best explanation among several possibilities. The best explanation is the one most likely to be true. The conclusion of the argument is that the preferred explanation is indeed probably true. For example:

ARGUMENT 22

Tariq flunked his philosophy course. The best explanation for his failure is that he didn't read the material. Therefore, he probably didn't read the material.

ARGUMENT 23

Ladies and gentlemen of the jury, the defendant was found with the murder weapon in his hand, blood on his clothes, and the victim's wallet in his pocket. We have an eyewitness putting the defendant at the scene of the crime. The best explanation for all these facts is that the defendant committed the murder. There can be very little doubt—he's guilty.

Here's the form of inference to the best explanation:

Phenomenon Q.

E provides the best explanation for Q.

Therefore, it is probable that E is true.

In any argument of this pattern, if the explanation given is really the best, then the argument is inductively strong. If the explanation is not the best, the argument is inductively weak. If the premises of the strong argument are true, then the argument is cogent. If the argument is cogent, then we have good reason to believe that the conclusion is true.

The biggest challenge in using inference to the best explanation is determining which explanation is the best. Sometimes this feat is easy. If our car has a flat tire, we may quickly uncover the best explanation for such a state of affairs. If we see a nail sticking out of the flat, and there is no obvious evidence of tampering or of any other extraordinary cause (that is, there are no good alternative explanations), we may safely conclude that the best explanation is that a nail punctured the tire.

In more complicated situations, we may need to do what scientists do to evaluate explanations, or theories—use special criteria to sort through the possibilities. Scientists call these standards the criteria of adequacy. Despite this fancy name, these criteria are basically just common sense, standards that you have probably used yourself.

One of these criteria is called *conservatism*. This criterion says that, all things being equal, the best explanation or theory is the one that fits best with what is already known or established. For example, if a friend of yours says—in all seriousness—that she can fly to the moon without using any kind of rocket or spaceship, you probably wouldn't believe her (and might even think that she needed psychiatric help). Your reasons for doubting her would probably rest on the criterion of conservatism—that what she says conflicts with everything science knows about space flight, human anatomy, aerodynamics, laws of nature, and much more. It is logically possible that she really can fly to the moon, but her claim's lack of conservatism (the fact that it conflicts with so much of what we already know about the world) casts serious doubt on it.

Here is another useful criteria for judging the worth of explanations: *simplicity*. Other things being equal, the best explanation is the one that is the simplest—that is, the one that rests on the fewest assumptions. The theory making the fewest assumptions is less likely to be false because there are fewer ways for it to go wrong. In the example about the flat tire, one possible (but strange) explanation is that space aliens punctured the tire. You probably wouldn't put much credence in this explanation because you would have to assume too many unknown entities and processes—namely, space aliens who have come from who knows where using who knows what methods to move about and puncture your tires. The nail-in-the-tire theory is much simpler (it assumes no unknown entities or processes) and therefore much more likely to be true.

Rule 2-3   Determine Whether the Premises Are True

When you are carefully reading an argument (whether in an essay or some other context), you will be just as interested in whether the premises are true as in whether the conclusion follows from the premises. If the writer is conscientious, he or she will try to ensure that each premise is either well supported or in no need of support (because the premise is obvious or agreed to by all parties). The needed support will come from the citing of examples, statistics, research, expert opinion, and other kinds of evidence or reasons. This arrangement means that each premise of the primary argument may be a conclusion supported in turn by premises citing evidence or reasons. In any case, you as the reader will have to carefully evaluate the truth of all premises and the support behind them.

When you are trying to write a good argument, the story will be much the same. You will want to provide good reasons to your readers for accepting the premises, for you understand that simply explaining your premises is not enough. You will have to provide support for each premise requiring it and ensure that the support is adequate and reliable. (See Chapter 6 for guidance on using and citing sources.)

APPLYING THE RULES

Let's read and evaluate an argument in an extended passage, applying the rules discussed in this chapter (as well as those in the last). The following excerpt focuses on one aspect of a famous argument for the existence of God. Read it and review the comments that follow.

The Design Argument
Nigel Warburton

1. One of the most frequently used arguments for God's existence is the Design Argument, sometimes also known as the Teleological Argument (from the Greek word *'telos'* which means 'purpose'). This states that if we look around us at the natural world we can't help noticing how everything in it is suited to the function it performs: everything bears evidence of having been designed. This is supposed to demonstrate the existence of [a] Creator. If, for example, we examine the human eye, we see how its minute parts all fit together, each part cleverly suited to what it was apparently made for: seeing. . . .

2. Even if, despite the objections mentioned so far, you still find the Design Argument convincing, you should notice that it doesn't prove the existence of a unique, all-powerful, all-knowing, and all-good God. Close examination of the argument shows it to be limited in a number of ways.

3. First, the argument completely fails to support monotheism—the view that there is just one God. Even if you accept that the world and everything in it clearly shows evidence of having been designed, there is no reason to believe that it was all designed by one God. Why couldn't it have been designed by a team of lesser gods working together? After all, most large-scale, complex human constructions such as skyscrapers, pyramids, space rockets, and so on, were made by teams of individuals, so surely if we carry the analogy to its logical conclusion it will lead us to believe that the world was designed by a group of gods.

4. Second, the argument doesn't necessarily support the view that the Designer (or designers) was all-powerful. It could plausibly be argued that the universe has a number of 'design faults': for instance, the human eye has a tendency to short-sightedness and to cataracts in old age—hardly the work of an all-powerful Creator wanting to create the best world possible. Such observations might lead some people to think that the Designer of the universe, far from being all-powerful, was a comparatively weak God or gods, or possibly a young god experimenting with his or her powers. Maybe the Designer died soon after creating the universe, allowing it to run down of its own accord. The Design Argument provides at least as much evidence for these conclusions as it does for the

existence of the God described by the Theists. So the Design Argument alone cannot prove that the Theists' God rather than some other type of God or gods exists.[1]

To be successful in evaluating the argument, we must approach the text with an open mind (Rule 1-1) and read actively and critically (Rule 1-2), striving for full understanding. After that, our top priority is to identify the conclusion and the premises (Rule 1-3) and then outline, paraphrase, or summarize the whole argument (Rule 1-4). Our ultimate task is to evaluate the argument and formulate a tentative judgment about it (Rule 1-5). And that means having a good understanding of different types of arguments (Rule 2-1) so we can determine whether the argument is valid or strong (Rule 2-2) and whether the premises are true (Rule 2-3).

After reading the excerpt a few times, we can see that the author's purpose is to present an argument against another argument, the so-called design argument. In paragraph 1, he explains that the design argument says that because everything in the world looks as though it has been designed, it must have a designer, namely God. But in paragraph 2, he asserts that the design argument doesn't prove what many people think it does. It doesn't prove that the designer is God in the traditional sense—an all-powerful, all-knowing, all-good supreme being. He backs up this assertion in paragraphs 3 and 4, giving two reasons for believing that the creator doesn't necessarily have to be anything like the traditional God.

After reading the excerpt, we should go back and look for indicator words. When we do, we find only one—the conclusion indicator word *So* in the last sentence of paragraph 4. The statement that *So* introduces is indeed the conclusion of the argument: "So the Design Argument alone cannot prove that the Theists' God [the traditional deity] rather than some other type of God or gods exists." This sentence, however, is a reiteration of the conclusion, which is also stated (in different words) for the first time in paragraph 2: "[The design argument] doesn't prove the existence of a unique, all-powerful, all-knowing, and all-good God."

After identifying the conclusion, we can see that the first premise must be in paragraph 3: "Even if you accept that the world and everything in it clearly shows evidence of having been designed, there is

[1]Excerpted from Chapter 1 of Nigel Warburton, *Philosophy: The Basics* (London: Routledge, 2000), 12, 14–15. Reproduced by permission of the publisher.

no reason to believe that it was all designed by one God." Perhaps the world was designed by many gods. The design argument gives us no reason to rule out this possibility.

The second premise, then, is in paragraph 4: "the [design] argument doesn't necessarily support the view that the Designer (or designers) was all-powerful." Perhaps the designer was weak, or inexperienced, or mortal. The design argument doesn't prove otherwise. When we outline the argument, we get this:

PREMISE 1: Even if you accept that the world and everything in it clearly shows evidence of having been designed, there is no reason to believe that it was all designed by one God.

PREMISE 2: The [design] argument doesn't necessarily support the view that the Designer (or designers) was all-powerful.

CONCLUSION: So the design argument alone cannot prove that the Theists' God rather than some other type of God or gods exist.

For the sake of clarity, we can paraphrase the argument:

PREMISE 1: The design argument doesn't show that the world must have been created by just one God.

PREMISE 2: The design argument doesn't show that world must have been created by an all-powerful God.

CONCLUSION: Therefore, the design argument doesn't show that the traditional God (all-powerful, all-knowing, and all-good) exists rather some other type of God or gods.

Now we ask the crucial question mandated by Rule 2-2: Does the conclusion follow from the premises? In this case, we would have to say yes. If the design argument fails to show that the creator is one God, and if it fails to show that the creator is all-powerful, then we must conclude that the design argument fails to show that the traditional God exists. That is, the author's argument is valid.

Next we ask the question prompted by Rule 2-3: Are the premises true? By studying the excerpt, we can see that the design argument, if strong, establishes only that the world probably had a designer (or designers). The argument does not show, however, that the designer had any distinguishing characteristics, including attributes associated with the traditional notion of God. If this is the case, then premise 1 must be true—the designer could have been one or many. Likewise, premise 2 must also be true—the designer could have been less than all-powerful.

Based on this analysis, we can say that the author's argument is sound. The design argument—in the form presented in our excerpt—does not prove the existence of a God with traditional attributes. Our analysis, however, is not the final word on the topic. There are other arguments relevant to the issues raised that we have not considered.

QUICK REVIEW: Basic Definitions

- *Statement:* An assertion that something is or is not the case. A statement is either true or false.

- *Argument:* A combination of statements in which some of them are intended to support another of them. Statements supposedly providing the support are the *premises;* the statement being supported is the *conclusion.*

- *Deductive argument:* An argument that is supposed to offer logically conclusive support for its conclusion. Deductive arguments can be *valid* or *invalid.* A valid argument with true premises is said to be *sound.*

- *Inductive argument:* An argument meant to offer probable support for its conclusion. Inductive arguments can be *strong* or *weak.* A strong argument with true premises is said to be *cogent.*

⊰ 3 ⊱

Rules of Style and Content for Philosophical Writing

Fortunately, there is much in the craft of essay writing that is the same no matter what your subject or purpose. To a comforting degree, writing is writing. There are matters of composition, grammar, punctuation, and usage (topics covered in Chapters 7 and 8) that must be attended to in every kind of essay you write.

Philosophical writing is no exception to this norm. Nonetheless, in some ways it is distinctive—or, as you may be tempted to say, peculiar. Some features of philosophical writing are characteristic of the genre, and some just take on much more importance than they might in many other types of expression. These features concern both content (what is said) and form (how it is said), and you must know how to handle them all if you are to write good philosophy essays.

For guidance, consider the following rules—and through practice learn how to competently apply them.

Rule 3-1   Write to Your Audience

Almost everything you write—from college papers to love notes—is intended for a particular audience. Knowing who your audience is can make all the difference in what you say and how you say it. Unless things have gone terribly awry, you would not ordinarily address members of the town council the same way you would your one true love, nor your one true love as you would readers of the *New England Journal of Medicine*. You may wonder, then, who is the intended audience of your philosophy paper?

Your instructor, of course, may specify your audience and thus settle the issue for you. Otherwise, you should assume that your audience consists of intelligent, curious readers who know little about philosophy but who are capable of understanding and appreciating a clearly written, well-made paper on many subjects, including philosophy. Unless you have instructions to the contrary, you should *not* assume that your audience consists of your instructor, professional philosophers generally, philosophy students who know more than you do, or readers who will either agree with everything you say or reject your thesis out of hand. Writing to your proper audience as defined here means that you will have to define unfamiliar terms, explain any points that may be misunderstood, and lay out your argument so that its structure and significance would be clear to any intelligent reader. This approach will both force you to attempt a better understanding of your subject and help you demonstrate this understanding through your writing.

If you know more about your readers than this general description would suggest, then you can tailor your essay to them even better. How much do your readers know about the issue? Are they adamantly opposed to your position? Are they mostly in agreement with you? How important is the issue to them? What common interests do you have with them? Can you expect your essay to change people's mind or just help them better appreciate or tolerate your view? Knowing the answers to any of these questions could change how you present your case.

Rule 3-2   Avoid Pretentiousness

Philosophy is profound, highbrow, and lofty; therefore, you should try to make your philosophy paper sound profound, highbrow, and lofty. Do you believe this? Some people who are new to philosophy do. They think that philosophical writing is supposed to sound grand, as if it were meant for God himself—or God's exalted servant, their instructor. This view is mistaken.

Good philosophy is often profound, but the profundity comes from the ideas or arguments expressed—not from fancy, overblown writing. Writing that tries to merely *seem* grand is said to be pretentious, and pretentious writing is bad writing whether composed by philosophers or philosophy students. (Alas, some philosophical writing is indeed pretentious.)

Pretentious writing is bad, in part, because it is empty. Like a pastry punctured by a fork, pretentious writing collapses when closely examined, proving that the outside is puffy while the inside has little substance. Philosophy papers are supposed to offer real arguments in support of a worthwhile conclusion. Intelligent readers (especially instructors) are likely to get annoyed or impatient when they discover that pretentious language is covering up a lack of argument or insight. It is far better to concentrate on presenting a good argument in plain, clear language.

Consider this passage:

Indubitably, the question as to whether utilitarianism can, through the utilization of a consideration of parameters that effectuate the amplification of life, liberty, and the pursuit of happiness for all who live and breathe in this earthly realm, enhance human happiness is of paramount importance.

This is pretentiousness gone wild, the cause of which is in plain sight. First, we meet several fancy words (with three to five syllables) that can be eliminated or replaced with simpler terms—*indubitably, utilization, parameters, effectuate, amplification,* and *paramount.* Second, the passage contains some unnecessarily ornate or lengthy phrases (some of which are also clichés)—*the question as to whether; life, liberty, and the pursuit of happiness;* and *all who live and breath in this earthly realm.* Third, the passage as a whole is pointlessly complex, an annoying problem that partially conceals the ordinariness of the passage's meaning.

Look at this version, with most of the pretentiousness and fuzziness removed:

Whether utilitarian principles can enhance human happiness is an important question.

We have thus gone from a sprawling, bombastic passage to a single, plain sentence without a significant loss in meaning. The new version is better. It is clear, straightforward—and does not pretend to be something it's not. (See Chapter 7 for related discussions on writing effective sentences.)

Rule 3-3   Keep the Authority of Philosophers in Perspective

In Chapter 6 we delve into the documentation of philosophy papers. This rule, however, addresses a related but separate issue: how to use the authority of philosophers in your papers.

As we have seen, it is legitimate to use evidence, including the testimony of experts, to support premises or conclusions in arguments, including arguments put forth in philosophy papers. You must be careful, however, when you try to back up your arguments by citing a philosopher. Remember that in philosophy, the world turns on arguments. Propositions and positions are advanced and challenged, accepted and rejected, based on the worth of relevant arguments. In a philosophical essay, the argument matters most, and the essential questions are whether the conclusion follows from the premises and whether the premises are true. Thus, if a philosopher—even a famous one—carries any weight in your essay, it is only because of his or her arguments. The mere fact that the philosopher is recognized as an authority (or is famous, reputable, or popular) cannot, by itself, have any bearing on whether a proposition is worthy of acceptance. So if you want to prove that all persons have free will, merely showing that a noted philosopher believes that all persons do cannot bolster your case one bit. Citing a good argument devised by the philosopher, however, can strengthen your case—because the argument is good, not because the argument comes from a particular philosopher. (As explained in Chapter 6, the source of any such reference, of course, must be properly documented.)

Rule 3-4   Do Not Overstate Premises or Conclusions

Overstatement is the problem of exaggerating claims, of making an assertion sound stronger or more inclusive than it deserves. We are all guilty of overstatement, most often in everyday speech. We may say, "Everyone dislikes Professor Jones" or "Americans think the French are snobbish" when in fact only *some* students dislike Professor Jones and only *a few* of our American friends think that *some* French people are snobbish. In everyday conversation, such exaggerations are often understood as such and are used innocuously for emphasis. But too often the overstatements are simply distortions, assertions that claim too much and lead us into error or prejudice. To a disconcerting degree, assertions regarding opposing views in religion, politics, and morality are overstatements. (See Chapter 5, especially discussions of the fallacies known as hasty generalization, slippery slope, and straw man.)

In philosophical essays, overstatement is never acceptable, and you must be on your guard against it. It can raise doubts in your readers about your judgment, your truthfulness, and your arguments. Even one overblown adjective or a single over-the-top phrase can undermine your credibility. Overstatement leads readers to think, "Here is an exaggeration; what else in this essay is exaggerated?"

In philosophical writing, overstatement arises in two ways. First, particular statements—including premises—can be exaggerated. You may be tempted to assert that whatever issue you are addressing in your essay is "the most important issue of our time." You might declare that a premise is certainly or undoubtedly true (when in fact it is merely probable) or forego important qualifiers such as "some," "perhaps," and "many." You may get carried away and say, for example, that killing another human being is *always* morally wrong, even though you would admit that killing in self-defense is morally permissible.

Second, the conclusions of arguments can be overstated: They can go beyond what logical inference would permit. As we saw in the previous chapter, a conclusion must follow from its premises. Because of your commitment to your conclusion, however, you may overstate it. The result is an invalid or weak argument.

Rule 3-5   Treat Opponents and Opposing Views Fairly

Sometimes it seems that most of what people know about arguing a position has been learned from the worst possible teachers—political debate–type television programs. In these forums, the standard procedure is to attack the character and motivations of opponents, distort or misrepresent opposing views, and dismiss opponents' evidence and concerns out of hand. This approach is neither condoned nor tolerated in philosophical writing. As we have seen, the ideal in philosophical discourse is the disinterested and fair-minded search for truth among all parties. Abusive or unfair tactics are out of order. They are also ineffective. When readers encounter such heavy-handedness, they are likely to be suspicious of the writer's motives, to wonder if the writer is close-minded, to question whether his or her assertions can be trusted, or to doubt the worth of arguments defended with such gratuitous zeal.

There are two ways that you can avoid most kinds of unfairness in your papers (both techniques are discussed in detail in Chapter 5):

1. Avoid the straw man fallacy.

2. Avoid the ad hominem fallacy.

The straw man fallacy consists of the distorting, weakening, or oversimplifying of someone's position so it can be more easily attacked or refuted. For example:

> The ACLU is opposed to school prayer because they want to force their secular, atheistic worldview down everyone's throat. They want the Supreme Court to forbid even silent, personal prayers of children who happen to be religious.

Here the ACLU and its views on school prayer are mischaracterized to make them seem ridiculous and easy to argue against. It is doubtful that the ACLU (or any other organization) wants to *force* Americans to abandon their religious beliefs. Likewise, the description of the ACLU's views in the second sentence is inaccurate. Even most religious organizations would not characterize the ACLU's stand on prayer in such a misleading way.

The point is that opposing views and arguments should be described fairly and accurately, acknowledging any strengths they have. This approach is likely to result in (1) your readers viewing you as more honest and conscientious and (2) your trying to find ways to address any weaknesses exposed in your own argument.

The ad hominem fallacy (also known as *appeal to the person*) consists of rejecting a claim on the grounds that there is something wrong not with the claim but with the person who makes it. Consider:

> You can't believe anything Jan says about the existence of souls. She's a philosophy major.

> We should reject the arguments put forth by the so-called great thinkers who think that there is such a thing as the rights of persons. Who cares what they think?

These arguments are baseless because they try to refute or undermine a claim by appealing to a person's character or motives. But a person's character or motives almost never have any bearing on a claim's worth. Claims must be judged by the reasons they have, or do not have, in their favor.

Rule 3-6 Write Clearly

Being clear is a matter of ensuring that your meaning is understood by the reader. In most kinds of writing, clarity is almost always a supreme virtue, and philosophical writing is no different. In fact, clarity in philosophical prose is arguably more important than in most other types of nonfiction because philosophy deals with so many difficult and unfamiliar ideas.

Lack of clarity in your writing can occur in several ways. Inexperienced writers often produce some very murky papers because too often they assume that because they know what they mean, others will know too. Typically, others do *not* know. The problem is that new writers have not yet developed the knack of viewing their own writing as others might. In other words, they fail to adopt an objective stance toward their own words. Good writers are their own best critics.

Trying to view your writing as others might takes practice. A trick that often helps is not to look at your writing for a day or two then go back to it and read it cold. You may discover after you take this little break that some passages that seemed clear to you earlier are mostly gibberish. Another technique is to use peer review. Ask a friend to read your paper and pinpoint any passages that seem unclear. Your friend doesn't have to know anything about philosophy. He or she just needs to be like your target audience—intelligent, curious, and able to appreciate what you're trying to do.

Ambiguity can also make writing less clear. A term or statement is ambiguous if it has more than one meaning (and the context doesn't help clear things up). Some ambiguities are *semantic;* they are the result of multiple meanings of a word or phrase. Consider the sentence, "Kids make nutritious snacks." The word *make* could mean *prepare* or *constitute.* If the former, the sentence says that kids can prepare food. If the latter, the sentence means that kids *are* food.

Some ambiguities are *syntactic;* they are the result of the way words are combined. Read this sentence straight through without stopping: "Maria saw the bird with binoculars." Who had the binoculars, Maria or the bird? We don't know because the sentence is poorly written; words are misplaced. If we want the sentence to say that Maria was the one holding the binoculars, we might rewrite it like this: "Using her binoculars, Maria saw the bird."

Often a lack of clarity comes not from ambiguous terms but from *vague* terms—words that fail to convey one definite meaning. This failure can be the result of many kinds of sloppiness, but at the head of the list is the tendency to use words that are too *general*. General words refer to whole groups or classes of things, such as *soldiers, artists,* and *books*. Specific words, on the other hand, refer to more particular items, such as *Sgt. Morris, van Gogh,* and *The Sun Also Rises.*

There is nothing inherently wrong with using general words; in fact, we *must* employ them in many circumstances, especially in philosophy. Used to excess, however, they can easily muddy a philosophy paper. Consider these pairs of sentences:

1. According to Hobbes, all persons are capable of free actions.

   According to Hobbes, all persons are capable of free actions. A free action is one that is caused by someone's will and that is not constrained by another person or some physical force or barrier.

2. In Kant's view of some aspects of human experience, there are conflicts between what moral considerations may lead us to conclude and acts in which one must aver a state of affairs that is contrary to fact.

   Kant believes that lying is always immoral.

At first glance, the first sentence in pair 1 may seem like a straightforward statement, but it is so general that it is almost mysterious. What is a *free action?* The second passage of the pair is much more specific. It reiterates the first sentence but elaborates on it, stipulating two conditions that must be met before an action can be considered a free action. Notice that the general statement was made more specific by adding more information—information that narrowed down the countless possibilities.

In pair 2, the first sentence is packed with general terms, including *aspects of human experience, moral considerations,* and *acts in which one must aver a state of affairs that is contrary to fact.* This sentence is an attempt to say what the second sentence says. The second sentence avoids as many generalities as possible and gets right to the point. The notion that lying is always immoral is, of course, a general principle, but there is much clarity to be gained by expressing it in more specific terms. Notice that in contrast to the first pair, the second pair of sentences obtained greater specificity by using fewer words, not more.

Writing a philosophy paper will always involve using general terms. The key is to make your writing as specific as your subject and purpose will allow. (See Chapters 7 and 8 for other ways to increase the clarity of your writing.)

Rule 3-7   Avoid Inappropriate Emotional Appeals

Emotional appeals in philosophical writing are almost always inappropriate and are usually considered elementary errors. Probably the worst offense is the substitution of emotion for arguments or premises. This ploy is a fallacy called, not surprisingly, *appeal to emotion*: the attempt to persuade someone of a conclusion not by offering a good argument but by trying to arouse the reader's feelings of fear, guilt, pity, anger, and the like. For example:

> Ladies and gentlemen of the jury, you must find my client not guilty. He is the unfortunate result of grinding poverty, a mother who rejected him, and a legal system that does not care that he was once a ragged, orphaned child wandering the streets in search of a single kind heart.

The appeal here is to pity, and the passage is shot through with language designed to evoke it—*grinding poverty, a mother who rejected him*, and *ragged, orphaned child*. But note: No good reasons are offered for believing that the defendant is innocent. No logical support at all is provided for this conclusion. If such an appeal were intended as the lone argument in a philosophy paper, the paper would have to be judged a failure.

Now consider this piece of political rhetoric:

> Dear voters, if you elect my opponent to the highest office in the land, will terrorist attacks on America increase? We cannot afford another September 11. Vote for security. Vote for me.

This is a blatant appeal to fear, a common tactic in politics. No good reasons are provided, just a very scary scenario.

Emotional appeals can seriously mislead the reader, even when they are not used as substitutes for arguments. By employing particular words or phrases that evoke strong emotions, a writer can powerfully influence the reader's attitudes and opinions. Look:

> The anti-life forces in this country that favor abortion—the murder of a child simply because he or she exists—are no better than the Nazis, who also exterminated millions of people simply because they existed and were inconvenient to the state. The

Machiavellian notion of abortion-on-demand should be replaced
with the enlightened pro-life view that life is better than death.

This passage is emotionally revved up to provoke outrage and
disgust—and the revving comes mostly from the use of a few powerfully evocative words. Word choice not only does most of the work,
but also enhances the effect of some fallacies. Ponder *anti-life, murder of a child, Nazis, exterminated millions, Machiavellian,* and *enlightened.* All these words are used misleadingly—and persuasively. Most
of them are used as part of a straw man argument, while some add
teeth to an ad hominem attack. (See Chapter 5.) Although the ma-
jority of emotive words are designed to cast abortion and abortion-
rights advocates in a bad light, the term *enlightened* is used to evoke
positive feelings about the pro-life side.

Five Common Mistakes in Philosophical Writing

1. Covering up a poor argument or lack of understanding with
   pretentious language.
2. Overstating your case.
3. Ridiculing opponents or opposing views.
4. Being guilty of the straw man fallacy.
5. Using emotional appeals.

Rule 3-8   Be Careful What You Assume

Behind every argument are presuppositions that need not be made
explicit because they are taken for granted by all parties. They may
be too obvious to mention or are in no need of justification. (They
are distinct from implicit premises, which are essential to an argument and should be brought out into the open.) In arguments about
the rights of hospital patients, for example, there would typically be
no need to explain that a hospital is not a Chevrolet truck, or that
patient rights have something to do with ethics, or that such rights
may be important to patients. You should, however, be careful not to
presuppose a claim that may be controversial among your readers. If
you wish to establish that abortion is morally permissible, you should
not assume your readers will agree that women have a right to choose
abortion or that a fetus is not a person.

Rule 3-9   Write in First Person

Unless your instructor tells you otherwise, use first person singular pronouns (*I, me, my, mine*). These are preferable to the more formal *we* ("*We* will show that . . .") or extremely formal and stilted locutions such as "It is to be noted that . . ." or "It is to be shown that. . . ." This advice correlates nicely with using the active voice (Rule 8-2) and taking full responsibility for the claims you make ("*I* contend that . . .").

Rule 3-10   Avoid Discriminatory Language

Sexist or racist language implies that a particular group of people is somehow not as good as other groups. This prejudicial way of speaking or writing can sneak into prose in several ways. Sometimes it happens when people refer to a group as if it were not really part of society as a whole. Some philosophers explain the problem like this:

> Some common ways of speaking and writing, for example, assume that "normal" people are all white males. It is still common practice, for instance, to mention a person's race, gender, or ethnic background if the person is not a white male, and not to do so if the person is. Thus, if we are talking about a white male from Ohio, we are apt to say simply, "He is from Ohio." But if the male is Latino, we might tend to mention that fact and say, "He is a Latino from Ohio"—even when the person's ethnic background is irrelevant to whatever we are taking about. This practice assumes that the "normal" person is not Latino and by implication insinuates that if you are, then you are "different" and a deviation from the norm, an outsider.
>
> Of course, it may be relevant to whatever you are writing about to state that this particular man is a Latino from Ohio and, if so, there is absolutely nothing wrong with writing "He is a Latino from Ohio."[1]

Unfortunately, some discriminatory tendencies are built into the English language. Traditionally, masculine pronouns have been used to refer to individuals even though they could be either male or female. For example:

A good scientist will always check *his* work.

Any CEO of a large corporation will work hard because *he* is conscientious.

[1]Brooke Noel Moore and Richard Parker, *Critical Thinking,* 6th ed. (Mountain View: Mayfield Publishing, 2001), 71.

Usually, the best remedy is either to use *both* masculine and feminine pronouns or to switch to the plural:

A good scientist will always check *his or her* work.

Good scientists will always check *their* work.

Any CEO of a large corporation will work hard because *he or she* is conscientious.

CEOs of large corporations will work hard because *they* are conscientious.

If this approach doesn't eliminate discriminatory wording, you may have to overhaul the whole sentence:

Scientific work should always be checked.

Conscientious CEOs of large corporations work hard.

QUICK REVIEW: Rules of Style and Content

Rule 3-1: Write to your audience.

Rule 3-2: Avoid pretentiousness.

Rule 3-3: Keep the authority of philosophers in perspective.

Rule 3-4: Do not overstate premises or conclusions.

Rule 3-5: Treat opponents and opposing views fairly.

Rule 3-6: Write clearly.

Rule 3-7: Avoid inappropriate emotional appeals.

Rule 3-8: Be careful what you assume.

Rule 3-9: Write in first person.

Rule 3-10: Avoid discriminatory language.

⚛ 4 ⚛

Defending a Thesis in an Argumentative Essay

In conversations, letters to the editor, or online discussions, have you ever taken a position on an issue and offered reasons why your view is correct? If so, then you have *defended a thesis.* You have presented an argument, giving reasons for accepting a particular thesis, or conclusion. If you elaborate on your argument in a written paper, you create something even more valuable—a *thesis defense* (or *argumentative*) *essay.*

In a thesis defense essay, you try to show the reader that your view is worthy of acceptance by offering reasons that support it. Your thesis may assert your position on a philosophical, social, or political issue; or on the arguments or claims of other writers (including some famous or not-so-famous philosophers); or on the interpretation of a single work or several. In every case, you affirm a thesis and give reasons for your affirmation.

This type of essay is not merely an analysis of claims, or a summary of points made by someone else, or a reiteration of what other people believe or say—although a good thesis defense essay may contain some of these elements. A thesis defense essay is supposed to be a demonstration of what *you* believe and *why* you believe it. What other people think is, ultimately, beside the point.

For many students, this kind of writing is unknown terrain. This land can only be traversed by thinking things through for themselves and by understanding claims and the reasons behind them—and students are seldom used to such a trip. The journey, however, is worthwhile and not entirely unfamiliar. In one form or another, you probably encounter thesis defense essays everyday. In advertising, political speeches, philosophical writing, letters to the editor, legal cases, special interest advocacy, press releases, position papers, and business communications of all kinds, you can see countless attempts to make a case for this view or that. Much of the world's work gets done this way (especially in the academic realm), and success or failure often depends on your ability to make your own case in writing or evaluate cases that come your way.

BASIC ESSAY STRUCTURE

Thesis defense essays usually contain the following elements, although not necessarily in this order:

I. Introduction (or opening)
    A. Thesis statement (the claim to be supported)
    B. Plan for the paper
    C. Background for the thesis
II. Argument supporting the thesis
III. Assessment of objections
IV. Conclusion

Introduction

The introduction often consists of the paper's first paragraph, sometimes just a sentence or two. Occasionally it is longer, perhaps several paragraphs. The length depends on how much ground you must cover to introduce the argument. Whatever the length, the introduction should be no longer than necessary. In most cases the best introductions are short.

If there is a rule of thumb for what the introduction must contain, it is this: The introduction should set forth the *thesis statement*. The thesis statement usually appears in the first paragraph. It is the claim that you hope to support or prove in your essay, the conclusion of the argument that you intend to present. You may want to pose the thesis statement as the answer to a question that you raise or as the solution to a problem that you wish to discuss. However presented, your thesis statement is the assertion you must support with reasons. It is like a compass to your readers, guiding them from paragraph to paragraph, premise to premise, showing them a clear path from introduction to conclusion. It also helps *you* stay on course. It reminds you to relate every sentence and paragraph to your one controlling idea.

In some argumentative essays—many newspaper editorials and magazine articles, for example—the thesis statement is not stated but is implied, just as in some arguments the premises or even the conclusion is implied. In philosophical writing, however, the thesis should always be explicit, asserted plainly in a carefully wrought sentence. Most likely, in any argumentative essay you write in college, you will be expected to include a thesis statement.

Your thesis statement should be restricted to a claim that you can defend in the space allowed. You want to state it in a single sentence and do so as early as possible. (More on how to devise a properly restricted thesis statement in a moment.) You may need to add a few words to explain or elaborate on the statement if you think its meaning or implications are unclear.

The other two parts of an introduction—the plan for the paper (B) and background information for the thesis (C)—may or may not be necessary, depending on your thesis and your intent. In more formal essays, you will need not only to state your thesis but also to spell out how you intend to argue for it. You will have to summarize your

---

How *Not* to Begin Your Philosophy Paper

Some starters are nonstarters. That is, student philosophy papers often begin poorly. They may open with a cliché, an irrelevant comment, an obvious or superfluous observation, or a long-winded lead-in to the thesis statement. Here are some examples:

- "Bertrand Russell [or some other philosopher] wrote many books."
- "From the beginning of time, people have wondered about. . ."
- "This paper will examine the ridiculous ideas of the atheist Jean-Paul Sartre."
- "The Bible tells us that . . ."
- "According to *Webster's Dictionary*, the word "necessity" means . . ."
- "As everyone knows, humans have free will . . ."

whole argument—each of your premises and conclusion—or, if your argument is long or complex, at least the most important points. Providing background information for your thesis is a matter of explaining what your thesis means (which includes defining terms and clarifying concepts), what its implications are, why the issue is so important or pressing, or why you have decided to address it. Sometimes the needed background information is so extensive that you must supply much of it after the introduction. At any rate, by adding the right kind of background information, you give your readers good reason to care about what you are saying and to continue reading.

In many philosophy papers, the background information includes a summary or sketch of the views of other philosophers—what they have said that is relevant to the issue or to your thesis. Providing this kind of material can help the reader understand why your topic is worth exploring and why your argument is relevant.

Argument Supporting the Thesis

Between your paper's introduction and conclusion is the *body* of the essay. The basic components of the body are (1) the premises of your argument plus the material that supports or explains them and (2) an evaluation of objections to your thesis. Each premise must be clearly stated, carefully explained and illustrated, and properly backed up by examples, statistics, expert opinion, argument, or other reasons or evidence. You may be able to adequately develop the essay by devoting a single paragraph to each premise, or you may have to use several paragraphs per premise.

Whatever tack you take, you must stick to the central rule of paragraph development: Develop just one main point in each paragraph, embodying that point in a topic sentence. Make sure that each paragraph in turn relates to your thesis statement.

If your essay is a critique of someone else's arguments, you should examine them in the body, explaining how they work and laying out the author's response to any major criticisms of them. Your account of the arguments should be accurate and complete, putting forth the author's best case and providing enough detail for your readers to understand the import of your own argument. After the presentation of the author's side of things, you can then bring in your critique, asserting and explaining each premise.

Some premises, of course, may be so obvious that they do not require support. The determining factor is whether your readers would be likely to question them. If your readers are likely to accept a premise as it is, no backup is required. If they are not, you need to support the premise. A common mistake is to assume that a premise would be accepted by everyone when in fact it is controversial (Rule 3-8).

In any case, you should present only your strongest premises. One weak premise can spoil the whole argument. To the reader, one flimsy premise is a reason to be suspicious of all the rest. It is better to include one good premise that you can support than five bad premises that are unsupportable.

Recall that in a good argument the conclusion logically follows from the premises, and the premises are true. Your task in the body of your essay is to put forth such an argument and to do so plainly—to clearly demonstrate to your readers that your premises are properly related to your conclusion and that they are true. You should leave no doubt about what you are trying to prove and how you are trying to prove it. In longer papers, you may want to back up your thesis with more than one argument. This is an acceptable way to proceed, providing you make the relationships between the separate arguments and your thesis clear.

Assessment of Objections

Very often an argumentative essay includes an *assessment of objections*—a sincere effort to take into account any objections or doubts that readers are likely to have about points in your essay. (In some cases, however, there may be no significant objections to assess, as is the case in the essay on cultural relativism in Chapter 1.) You must show your readers that the objections are unfounded, that your argument is not fatally wounded by likely criticisms. Contrary to what some may think, when you deal effectively with objections in your essay, you do not weaken it—you strengthen it. You lend credibility to it by making an attempt to be fair and thorough. You make your position stronger by removing doubts from your readers' minds. If you don't confront likely objections, your readers may conclude either that you are ignorant of the objections or that you don't have a good reply to them. An extra benefit is that in dealing with objections, you may see ways to make your argument stronger.

On the other hand, you may discover that you do not have an adequate answer to the objections. Then what? Then you look for ways to change your arguments or thesis to overcome the criticisms. You can weaken your thesis by making it less sweeping or less probable.

Or you may need to abandon your thesis altogether in favor of one that is stronger. Discovering that your beloved thesis is full of holes is not necessarily a setback. You have increased your understanding by finding out which boats will float and which will not.

You need not consider every possible objection, just the strongest ones. You might use objections that you have come across in your reading and research, or heard from others, or just dreamed up on your own. Whatever you do, do not select pseudo-objections—those that you know are weak and easily demolished. Careful readers (including your instructor!) will see through this game and will think less of your paper.

Where in your paper you bring up objections can vary. You may choose to deal with objections as you go along—as you present each of your premises. On the other hand, you may want to handle objections at the beginning of the essay or near the end after defending the premises.

Conclusion

Unless your essay is very short, it should have a *conclusion*. The conclusion usually appears in the last paragraph. Many conclusions simply reiterate the thesis statement and then go on to emphasize how important it is. Others issue a call to action, present a compelling perspective on the issue, or discuss further implications of the thesis statement. Some conclusions contain a summary of the essay's argument. A summary is always a good idea if the argument is complex, long, or formal.

A Well-Built Essay

How might all of these parts fit together to make an essay? To find out, read the brief paper by Kathleen Moore[1] and review the comments that follow. You will see that although it is short and structurally simple, it has all the major elements that longer and more complex essays do. (There are no references to the paper's sources here, something that would normally be included in such an essay. We explore documentation styles in Chapter 6.)

---

[1]"Should Relatively Affluent People Help the Poor?" by Kathleen Dean Moore, following an outline written by her student, Brian Figur. Reproduced by permission of Kathleen Dean Moore.

Should Relatively Affluent People Help the Poor?

Kathleen Moore

1 As the world approaches the end of the twentieth century, the gap between rich and poor has never been wider. While some people have more money than it is possible to spend in a lifetime, no matter how lavishly they might make purchases, others are not able to provide even for their most basic needs. On all the continents of the world, people starve to death for lack of food, freeze to death for lack of shelter, die of diseases that could be prevented. The situation raises the issue of whether the affluent people of the world have a moral obligation to help the poor. I shall argue that people who are relatively affluent should give a certain fair percentage of their earnings to help reduce absolute poverty on a global scale.

Introduces topic, provides background.

Imparts a sense of urgency to issue.

Thesis statement.

2 My claim is that those who are relatively affluent, that is, people who would normally be defined as rich or wealthy in the context of a given society, have an obligation to give up a small but helpful percentage of their earnings. Peter Singer, an Australian philosopher, suggests ten percent. The money would be used to alleviate absolute poverty, a condition that Robert McNamara, the former president of the World Bank, defines as "characterized by malnutrition, illiteracy, disease, squalid

Defines relevant terms.

Source is quoted.

Normally an endnote would go at end of this quotation.

surroundings, high infant mortality and low life expectancy that is beneath
any reasonable definition of human decency."

3 Many people argue that wealthy people should not have to help *Body of paper begins here.* those who are needier than they, unless they choose to do so. The
strongest argument for this claim is articulated by Garrett Hardin, an
ecologist from the University of Southern California. He points to the

writer paraphrases critic.

harmful results of helping people, claiming that by contributing to the *Writer explains objections to her thesis in this paragraph.* increased survival rates of those who would otherwise have a relatively
low life expectancy, wealthier people would increase the world's
population and thus increase the rate at which natural resources are
consumed and environmental problems arise. Although starvation is an

An endnote would go at the end of this sentence.

evil, Hardin says, helping the poor would create an even greater evil—
increased numbers of starving people and fewer resources to help them.
Others argue that just because affluent people have a relatively higher
income than others, it does not follow that they are morally responsible for
those who do not.

4 I believe, in contrast, that people do have a moral obligation to *Writer launches counterarguments here.* help the desperately poor. For several reasons, it is not the case that
helping the poor would necessarily increase population and thus increase
environmental degradation. First, while monetary aid could bring medical
supplies and food and thus increase population, it could also bring
contraceptive devices and increased education about population control.
And so, helping the poor could actually decrease the rate of population

3

growth and, in the end, save environmental resources. Secondly, helping to reduce absolute poverty would also bring about more people who would be in a position economically, socially, and medically to contribute to cleaning up environmental problems and helping solve overpopulation problems. Finally, from a purely practical point of view, it is important to note that people are an economic resource at least as important as firewood and fertile soil, and to allow people to sicken and die is to spoil and waste that resource.

Here is first argument for thesis.

5 The obligation to help the poor is, to a certain extent, simply a matter of human rights. We believe that our pets have a right to decent treatment—enough food to live, shelter from the cold, medical care when they are hurt or ill, and affluent people in America spend large amounts of income to provide for these basic needs for animals. If animals have these rights, then surely humans have at least the same basic rights. People should be treated with more respect and consideration than animals by being given the chance to live in better surroundings than those afforded to animals.

Here is second argument for thesis.

6 However, the primary reason why the affluent have an obligation to help the poor has to do with the moral principle that killing another human being is wrong. If it is wrong to kill another person, then it is also morally wrong to allow someone to die, when you know they are going to die otherwise, and when it is within your means to save their lives at relatively little cost to yourself. By not acting to reduce the harmful, lethal

4

effects of poverty on the world's poor, affluent people are violating a primary moral principle. Therefore, it is a moral responsibility of the rich to help the poor.

7 In conclusion, affluent people should give a certain percentage of their wealth to help do away with absolute poverty in the world, because people are not only living beings who have a right to decent lives, but because it is wrong to allow people to die when helping them live is well within your means.

The paper's conclusion and a restatement of the thesis.

The introduction of this essay is laid out in paragraphs 1 and 2. *Paragraph 1* introduces the topic: the gap between rich and poor and whether the more affluent have a moral obligation to help narrow that gap. Background information includes the observation that the gap is wider than ever and that people all over the world are dying as a result of extreme poverty. These points impart a sense of urgency regarding the problem and help explain why the author thinks the issue matters and why the reader should care. The thesis statement is expressed in the last sentence of paragraph 1: "people who are relatively affluent should give a certain fair percentage of their earnings to help reduce absolute poverty on a global scale."

Paragraph 2 provides further background in the form of some definitions of key terms. "Relatively affluent," the writer says, means "rich or wealthy in the context of a given society." She cites philosopher Peter Singer's definition of a "fair percentage" of earnings—10 percent. To define "absolute poverty," she quotes Robert McNamara, someone who presumably has the proper credentials to offer an authoritative opinion. Absolute poverty, he says, is a condition "characterized by malnutrition, illiteracy, disease, squalid surroundings, high infant mortality and low life expectancy that is beneath any reasonable definition of human decency."

The body of the paper begins in *paragraph 3*, where the writer explains the objections to her thesis. Discussing the objections early is a good strategy when they are thought to be especially strong or foremost in the reader's mind. Dispatching them promptly prepares the way for the writer's own arguments. In many papers, however, objections are dealt with *after* the writer puts forth his or her own arguments.

In *paragraph 3* the writer describes two objections in the form of arguments, one of which she considers the strongest against her position. Her approach is exactly right. Dealing with the most robust objection you can find will actually strengthen your case. On the other hand, to pick a weak objection to demolish is to lapse into the straw man fallacy, almost a guarantee that your argument will not be as strong as it could be (Rule 3-5). Moreover, in this situation, the strongest objection has been offered previously by a knowledgeable critic and is part of a real-world controversy.

The strongest argument against the thesis says that rich people have no moral obligation to aid the poor because helping them would actually *increase* the number of starving people in the world. Helping the poor would only multiply their numbers, raising the world's population while diminishing its population-sustaining resources. The second argument takes another tack: From the mere fact that the wealthy are relatively better off than others, it does not follow that they have a moral obligation to share their prosperity with those less fortunate.

After detailing the arguments against her thesis, in *paragraph 4* the writer immediately launches a counterargument to show that aiding the poor would not necessarily multiply their numbers and their misery. Her three premises are: (1) Although giving money to help the poor might increase their population, it might also diminish it by providing them with methods of contraception and educating them about population control. (2) Reducing absolute poverty would shrink the world's population by increasing the number of people who have the wherewithal to help curb population growth and environmental harm. (3) People themselves are economic resources that can be used for the benefit of the world.

Notice that the writer does not immediately respond to the second argument against her thesis ("From the mere fact that the wealthy are relatively better off than others, it does not follow that they have a moral obligation to share their prosperity with those less fortunate.") That is, she does not try right away to show that its conclusion is false. She instead counters the argument later when she presents her case for her thesis. She shows, in effect, that contrary to the opposition's second argument, the wealthy do indeed have an obligation to share their prosperity with the poor.

After handling the main objection to her thesis, the writer articulates two arguments that support it. In *paragraph 5*, she holds that aid to the poor can be justified by an appeal to human rights. She argues that: (1) If animals have a right to decent treatment, then surely people have at least the same right. (2) Animals do have a right to decent treatment. (3) Therefore, people have a right to at least the same level of treatment (and in fact have a right to even better treatment).

In *paragraph 6*, she puts forth another argument that she believes is even more important than the preceding one: (1) It is wrong to kill another person. (2) If it is wrong to kill another person, it is wrong to allow a person to die (if you can easily prevent the death). (3) If the wealthy fail to decrease absolute poverty (something they can easily do), they allow poor people to die. (4) Therefore, it is wrong for the wealthy to not help the poor (they have a moral obligation to help).

Paragraph 7 presents the essay's conclusion, summarizing what the arguments (and counterarguments) have shown: Wealthy people should help reduce absolute poverty.

An outline of the essay's arguments would look like this:

OBJECTION I

UNSTATED PREMISE: If helping the poor would actually increase the number of starving people in the world, rich people should not help the poor.

PREMISE: Helping the poor would actually increase the number of starving people in the world.

CONCLUSION: Therefore, rich people have no moral obligation to aid the poor.

OBJECTION 2

PREMISE: From the mere fact that the wealthy are relatively better off than others, it does not follow that they have a moral obligation to share their prosperity with those less fortunate.

CONCLUSION: Therefore, it does not follow that the wealthy have a moral obligation to share their prosperity with those less fortunate.

RESPONSE TO OBJECTION I

PREMISE: Although giving money to help the poor might increase their population, it might also diminish it by providing them with methods of contraception and educating them about population control.

PREMISE: Reducing absolute poverty would shrink the world's population by increasing the number of people who have the wherewithal to help curb population growth and environmental harm.

PREMISE: People themselves are economic resources that can be used for the benefit of the world.

CONCLUSION: Therefore, aiding the poor would not necessarily increase their numbers and their misery.

FIRST ARGUMENT FOR THESIS (AND RESPONSE TO OBJECTION 2)

PREMISE: If animals have a right to decent treatment, then surely people have at least the same right.

PREMISE: Animals do have a right to decent treatment.

CONCLUSION: Therefore, people have a right to at least the same level of treatment that animals have (and in fact have a right to even better treatment).

SECOND ARGUMENT FOR THESIS (AND RESPONSE TO OBJECTION 2)

PREMISE: It is wrong to kill another person.

PREMISE: If it is wrong to kill another person, it is wrong to allow a person to die (if you can easily prevent the death).

PREMISE: If the relatively affluent fail to decrease absolute poverty (something they can easily do), they allow poor people to die.

CONCLUSION: Therefore, it is wrong for the relatively affluent not to decrease absolute poverty (they have a moral obligation to help the poor).

MAIN CONCLUSION

CONCLUSION: Therefore, the relatively affluent have a moral obligation to decrease absolute poverty (help the poor).

In this outline you can see that the conclusions to the first and second arguments for the thesis are, essentially, the main premises for the essay's main argument, whose conclusion is "Therefore, the relatively affluent have a moral obligation to decrease absolute poverty (help the poor)."

WRITING THE ESSAY: STEP BY STEP

Now we examine the steps involved in crafting a good thesis defense essay. You have the best chance of writing a good essay if you try to follow these steps. Just remember that the process is not linear. You may not be able to follow the steps in the sequence suggested. You may have to backtrack or rearrange the order of the steps. This kind of improvising on the fly is normal—and often necessary. At any stage in the process, you may discover that your argument is not as good as you thought, or that you did not take an important fact into account, or that there is a way that you can alter the essay to make it stronger. You may then want to go back and rework your outline or tinker with the draft you are working on—and your essay will be better for it. Rethinking and revising are normal procedures for even the best writers.

Here are the steps:

1. Select a topic and narrow it to a specific issue.
2. Research the issue.

3. Write a thesis statement.
4. Create an outline.
5. Write a first draft.
6. Study and revise your first draft.
7. Produce a final draft.

Step I   Select a Topic and Narrow It to a Specific Issue

This step is first for a reason. It is here to help inexperienced writers avoid a tempting but nasty trap: picking a thesis out of the air and writing their paper on it. Caution: Any thesis that you dream up without knowing anything about it is likely to be unusable—and a waste of time. It is better to begin by selecting a topic or issue and narrowing it through research and hard thinking to a manageable thesis.

A topic is simply a broad category of subject matter, such as *human cloning*, *space exploration*, *capital punishment*, and *stem-cell research*. Within topics lurk an infinite number of issues—that is, questions that are in dispute. From the topic of capital punishment, for example, countless issues arise: whether executing criminals deters crime, whether executing a human being is ever morally permissible, whether it is ethical to execute people who are insane or mentally impaired, whether the system of capital punishment in the United States is unfair, whether the death penalty should be mandatory for serial killers, whether executing juveniles is immoral . . . the list could go on and on. The basic idea is to select from the roster of possibilities an issue that (1) you are interested in and (2) you can adequately address in the space allowed.

Here are some issues under the topic of "God" that could be adequately addressed in a 750- to 1,000-word paper:

- Is Anselm's ontological argument for the existence of God sound?
- Should the phrase "under God" be removed from the Pledge of Allegiance if its recitation is required of public school children?
- Does the Big Bang argument prove that God exists?
- Should belief in God be a requirement for being president of the United States?

- Does William Paley's argument from design show that God exists?

- Can someone who does not believe in God behave morally?

- Does belief in God cause terrorism?

And here are some issues whose scope is too broad to adequately deal with in a short paper:

- Does God exist?

- Are religion and science compatible?

- Does the existence of evil show that there is no God?

Step 2   Research the Issue

The main reason for researching an issue is to find out what view-points and arguments are involved. Often your instructor will suggest good sources to research for a particular writing assignment. Your as-signed reading may be the only source you need to check. Otherwise, you can read articles and books, talk to people who have studied the issue or at least thought about it carefully, or go online to review top-ical or philosophical sites.

Let's say you begin with this issue: whether religion and contempo-rary morality conflict or complement each other. You probably can see right away that this issue is much too broad to be handled in a short (or long!) paper. You can restrict the scope of the issue, however—to, for example, whether a supreme being is the foundation of moral val-ues, a perennial question in the philosophy of religion.

Now you can explore viewpoints and arguments on all sides of the issue. You may not be able to examine *every* relevant argument, but you can probably inspect the strongest or most common ones, in-cluding some that you invent yourself. In your assessment, you want to determine what the premises are, how they relate to the conclu-sion, and whether they are true. (Remember, one of the best ways to test an argument is to outline it, using complete sentences, with the premises and conclusion stated as clearly as possible.) The point is to uncover a *good* argument—and one worth writing and reading about. (Refer to Rules 1-3, 1-4, 2-2, and 2-3.)

The evaluation process is much the same if you decide to use more than one argument to support your thesis. The conclusion of each argument would be used in support of the thesis, just as the premises of each argument would support its conclusion. The challenge is to ensure that the connections between all the parts of the essay are clear and logical.

Suppose you narrow the God-and-morality issue to a question about the divine command theory, the popular view that God is the foundation of morality (that an action is right if God commands it to be so). An outline of an argument against the theory might look like this:

PREMISE 1: If an action is right only because God commands it (that is, nothing is right or wrong in itself), then God's commands would be arbitrary.

PREMISE 2: If an action is right only because God commands it (that is, nothing is right or wrong in itself), then abhorrent actions would be right if God commanded them.

PREMISE 3: If the implications of the theory are implausible, then the theory is implausible.

CONCLUSION: Therefore, the theory is implausible and should be rejected.

Step 3   Write a Thesis Statement

The conclusion of your selected argument will serve as the basis for your thesis statement. Often the conclusion *is* your thesis statement. Writing a good thesis statement is an essential step because the entire essay is built on it. An imprecise or clumsy thesis statement can lead to an imprecise or clumsy argument, which can wreck any argumentative essay.

At this stage, you should try to get the wording of your statement just right, even though you may revise it later on. Its scope should be *restricted* to what you can handle in the space you have. It should also be *focused* on just one idea, not several. It should assert, for example, that "Mandatory sentencing guidelines for judges result in many miscarriages of justice," *not* "Mandatory sentencing guidelines for judges result in many miscarriages of justice, and the U.S. Senate should approve more judicial appointments." This latter thesis makes two claims, not one. A good thesis statement must also be *clear*. No one should have to guess about the meaning of your thesis. The thesis "Same-sex marriages are intolerable," for example, is intolerably vague since there are many ways that something can be intolerable. It gives us very little information about what will be discussed in the essay.

It is possible to devise a thesis statement that is restricted, focused, clear—and trivial. A trivial thesis statement is one that either concerns an insignificant issue or makes an insignificant claim. People generally don't care about insignificant issues, and few would bother to disagree with an insignificant claim. Who cares whether pens are better than pencils or whether gambling is more fun than beachcombing? And who would care to contest the claim that pleasure is better than pain? An essay built on a trivial thesis statement wastes your readers' time (if they bother to read it at all), and you learn nothing and change nothing by writing it. Thesis statements should be *worthy*.

Here are some thesis statements that meet these criteria:

- Jeremy Bentham's moral theory known as act-utilitarianism conflicts with our commonsense ideas about human rights.

- The U.S. government should be allowed to arrest and indefinitely imprison without trial any American citizen who is suspected of terrorism.

- Subjective relativism—the view that truth depends on what someone believes—is self-refuting.

- Racial profiling should not be used to do security screening of airline passengers.

- The city of Cincinnati should be allowed to ban art exhibits if they are deemed anti-religious or blasphemous.

Step 4   Create an Outline of the Whole Essay

If you can write out your thesis statement and outline the argument used to defend it, you have already come far. Your argument and thesis statement will constitute the skeleton of your essay. The next step is to flesh out the bones with introductory or explanatory material, responses to objections, and support for the premises (which may consist of subordinate arguments, examples, explanations, analogies, statistics, scientific research, expert opinion, or other evidence). Producing a detailed, coherent outline of the whole essay is the best way to manage this task, and if you already have an outline of your argument, creating an outline for the whole essay will be easy. An outline helps you fill out your argument in an orderly fashion, showing you how the pieces fit together and whether any parts are missing or misaligned. This filling-out process will probably require you to research your thesis further—to check the truth of premises, examine alternative arguments, look for additional evidence, or assess the strength of objections to your argument.

Do not be afraid to alter your outline at any stage. As you write, you may realize that your thesis is weak, your argument flawed, or your premises vague. If so, you should go back and adjust the outline before writing any further. Writing is an act of exploration, and good writers are not afraid to revise when they find something amiss.

When you outline your essay, include your full thesis statement in the introduction. Then as you work on the outline, you can refer to the statement for guidance. The major points of your outline will include the premises, conclusion, objections, and responses to objections. Here, for example, is a preliminary outline for the divine command essay.

I. INTRODUCTION: (Thesis) The divine command theory is implausible and should be rejected.

   A. Explanation of theory.

   B. Socrates's dilemma.

II. FIRST PREMISE: If an action is right only because God commands it (that is, nothing is right or wrong in itself), then God's commands would be arbitrary—an implausible result.

   A. According to the theory, if God commands murder, then murder is right.

   B. God can command anything because he is all powerful.

III. SECOND PREMISE: If an action is right only because God commands it (that is, nothing is right or wrong in itself), then abhorrent actions would be right if God commanded them—another implausible result.

IV. OBJECTION: God would not command evil actions because he is all good.

   A. Response: The objection begs the question.

   B. Response: Rachels's version of the question-begging response.

V. THIRD PREMISE: If the implications of the theory are implausible, then the theory is implausible.

VI. CONCLUSION: Therefore, the theory is implausible and should be rejected.

Notice that this outline indicates where objections will be addressed. Objections lodged against individual premises (and responses to them) should be shown on the outline as subpoints under the main premise divisions. Objections that are handled in one place in the body of the essay should be indicated as another major point with a Roman numeral.

Ten Common Mistakes in Argumentative Essays

1. Failing to evaluate and revise a first draft.
2. Assuming that anyone's opinion is as good as anyone else's.
3. Formulating a thesis that's too broad.
4. Assuming that the reader can read your mind.
5. Overstating what has been proven.
6. Failing to start the paper early enough so there's time for evaluation and revisions.
7. Attacking an author's character instead of his or her argument.
8. Presenting unsupported assertions instead of good arguments.
9. Padding the essay with irrelevant or redundant passages.
10. Using quotes from authors in place of well-developed arguments.

Your outline should also reveal how you intend to provide support for premises that need it. This level of detail can help you head off any unpleasant surprises in the writing phase.

In many cases, the points and subpoints in your outline may correspond to the topic sentences for your essay's paragraphs. In this way, a detailed outline (in which each point is a complete sentence) can almost write your essay for you—or at least make the writing much easier.

You will find that as you tweak the outline, you may need to adjust the thesis statement. And as you perfect the thesis statement, you may need to adjust the outline. In the end, you want to satisfy yourself that the outline is complete, accurate, and structurally sound, tracing a clear and logical progression of points.

Step 5   Write a First Draft

Good writers revise . . . and revise and revise. They either write multiple drafts, revising in successive passes, or they revise continuously as they write. They know that their first tries will always be in need of improvement. Inexperienced writers, on the other hand, too often dash off a first draft without a second look—then turn it in! A much more reasonable approach (and the best one for most students) is to at least write a first draft and a final draft or—better—several drafts and a final one.

In argumentative essays, because of the importance of articulating an argument carefully and the difficulty of writing later drafts of the essay unless the first one is in reasonable shape, the first draft should be fairly solid. That is, in your first draft, you should write a tentative version of each paragraph, and the wording of your thesis statement and all premises should be at least close to final form.

Give your draft a good introduction that lays out your thesis statement, provides background information on the issue, and draws your readers into the essay. Make it interesting, informative, and pertinent to the question at hand. Do not assume that your readers will automatically see that your paper is worth reading.

A common problem with student papers is wordy and superficial introductions—those that go on and on about the topic but say little that is germane or necessary. Such intros read as if they are either just filling up space or slowly warming up to the subject. They can often be deleted entirely without any loss to the essay because the true introduction begins on page 3. The best introductions are concise, relevant—and, usually, short.

In a less formal essay, you can grab the attention of your readers and lead them into the paper by starting off with a bold statement of your thesis, a provocative scenario that encapsulates or symbolizes the issue, or a compelling fact suggesting the importance of your thesis.

In a more formal paper, the usual course is to assert your thesis statement, spell out the issue, and explain how you plan to develop your argument or how the rest of the essay will unfold (without going into lengthy detail). In short papers, you can mention every premise; in long or complex essays, just stating the most important points should suffice.

Look at this introduction to the divine command essay (presented in its entirety later in this chapter):

1. Many people believe that God is a lawgiver who alone defines what actions are right and wrong. God, in other words, is the author of morality; an action is right if and only if God commands it to be done. According to this view, there is no right or wrong until God says so, and nothing is moral or immoral independently of God's willing it to be thus. God, and only God, makes rightness and wrongness. This view is known as the divine command theory of morality.

2. A simple version of the theory is widely accepted today, among both the religious and nonreligious. In this version, God is thought to be the source of all moral principles and values. He can be the source of all morality because he is omnipotent, being able to do anything whatsoever, including create the very foundations of right and wrong.

3. In the *Euthyphro*, Socrates brings out what is probably the oldest and strongest criticism of the theory. He asks, in effect, is an action right because God commands it to be done, or does God command it to be done because it is right? This question lays bare the dilemma that is inherent in the theory: If an action is right because God commands it, then there is nothing in the action itself that makes it right, and God's command is arbitrary. If God commands the action because it is right (that is, he does not make it right), then rightness would seem to be independent of (or prior to) God, and the divine command theory is false. I contend that, at least in the simplest version of the theory, this ancient dilemma still stands and that the most plausible way to resolve it is to reject the theory by accepting that moral standards must exist independently of God's commands.

This introduction is long because the issue requires considerable explanation and background. The key question of the essay, however, is raised almost immediately in the first paragraph: Does God make rightness? In paragraphs 2 and 3, the writer explains the divine command theory so that its controversial status is evident and its relevance to current views on morality is clear. After all, a version of the theory is "widely accepted today," and the question of its truth was raised by none other than Socrates. The thesis statement appears in the last sentence of paragraph 3: "Moral standards must exist independently of God's commands."

The body of your essay should state, explain, and develop your argument in full. You should present each premise, elaborate on it as necessary, and provide support for it if it is likely to be questioned by readers. Plan on devoting at least one paragraph to each premise, although many more may be needed to make your case.

Every paragraph in your paper should relate to the thesis; every sentence in each paragraph should relate to a topic sentence. Delete any sentence that does not serve the essay's purpose. Ensure that paragraphs appear in a logical sequence and are clearly linked by transitional words and phrases or references to material in preceding paragraphs. Your readers should never have to wonder what the connection is between parts of your paper.

These two paragraphs follow the introduction:

4. The central argument against the notion that rightness is whatever God commands is this: If an action is right only because God commands it (that is, nothing is right or wrong in itself, or independent of God), then cruelty, murder, torture, and many other terrible actions would be right if God commanded them. If God commanded such acts, then they would be right, and no one would be committing a wrong by doing them. On the simple version of the theory, there are no limits whatsoever to God's power, so he could indeed command such things. If nothing would be right or wrong until God wills it, he could have no reason to either command murder or forbid it, to sanction the torture of innocents or prohibit it. Therefore, if God commands rightness, God's commands would be arbitrary—a result that would be implausible to the religious and non-religious alike.

5. A parallel argument is also possible. As stated above, if an action is right only because God commands it, then cruelty, murder, torture, and many other terrible actions would be right if God commanded them. This means that such immoral actions—immoral in light of common moral standards—could be transformed by God into moral actions. This outcome, however, would also be implausible to both the religious and nonreligious.

This essay presents two separate arguments to support its thesis statement—one in paragraph 4 and one in paragraph 5. Paragraph 4 argues that if God commands (makes) rightness, then his commands are arbitrary, a point expressed in the topic sentence (the last one in the paragraph). Paragraph 5 argues that if God commands rightness, he could make immoral actions moral, and this too is implausible. This argument also appears in the paragraph's topic sentence (the sentence beginning "This means that . . .").

The connection between the statements in paragraph 4 and those in paragraph 5 is apparent. The transitional sentence in paragraph 5

("A parallel argument is also possible") helps bridge the gap between the paragraphs.

In most cases, your essay will need a conclusion. It may simply reiterate the thesis statement (without repeating it word for word). In long, formal, or complex papers, the conclusion may include a summary of the essay's arguments. In short or simple essays, there may be no need for a conclusion; the point of the whole essay may be evident and emphatic without a conclusion. If you are unsure whether your paper needs a conclusion, take no chances: Include one.

The conclusion, however, is not the place to launch into a completely different issue, make entirely unsubstantiated claims, malign those who disagree with you, or pretend that your argument is stronger than it really is. These tacks will not strengthen your essay but weaken it.

Step 6   Study and Revise Your First Draft

Your first draft is likely to have problems both big and small. At this stage, however, you should scrutinize mostly the big ones. This is no time for proofreading (correcting spelling, fixing punctuation, repairing typos, and the like). This is the time to make substantive changes such as those listed here. Put your paper aside for a while, then read it critically and do the following:

- *Examine your argument first.* Check to see that the premises are properly related to the conclusion and that they are adequately supported. Ask: Does the conclusion follow from the premises? Are the premises true? Is the supporting evidence solid? Would a reader be convinced by this argument? Rewrite the argument, or parts of it, if need be.

- *Check for unity.* Make sure that every paragraph relates to the thesis statement and discusses just one idea. Delete or modify paragraphs and sentences that go off on tangents. Remove any padding, passages that are irrelevant to the essay but are inserted to lengthen the paper or make it seem more impressive.

- *Test for clarity.* As you read the paper, ask yourself: Is the thesis stated clearly? Does the paper's introduction tell the reader what the essay is about and how the argument will unfold? Do the topic sentences need to be more explicit? Are there points that need to be emphasized more? Are ideas and premises adequately explained? Are the connections among ideas clear? Are there appropriate transitions to keep readers on track? Revise for maximum clarity.

- *Hunt for repetitions.* Look for phrasing in which you have repeated ideas or words unnecessarily. Are you just repeating yourself rather than fully developing your points? Cut out or rewrite suspect passages.

- *Think your paper through.* Ask yourself if you are really *engaged* in the critical thinking required to produce a good paper. Are you just repeating what your sources say without fully understanding them? Are you assuming, without checking, that certain statements are true? Are you ignoring contrary evidence or contradictions? Are you going for the obvious and the simplistic when you should be trying to address complexity?

- *Smooth out the language.* Fix awkward sentences, grammatical errors, wordy constructions, pretentious phrasing, and other impediments to clear communication. (See Chapters 7 and 8.)

- *Show your draft to others.* Even if those who read your paper know little about philosophy, they should be able to understand your thesis statement, your argument, and all important points. They should be able to tell from the introduction exactly what you are trying to do in your paper. If any part of the essay is confusing to them, consider rewriting that passage.

After writing and revising your first draft, repeat the process, creating as many drafts as necessary. Your goal is to revise until you have made all the necessary substantive changes.

Step 7   Produce a Final Draft

After completing all substantive changes, you should generate a final draft, the one you will turn in. The final draft should reflect not only the big changes, but also the corrections of all minor errors as well—misspellings, typos, grammatical errors, misplaced words, faulty punctuation, and documentation mistakes. This task should be primarily a proofreading job. At this stage, you should also format the manuscript according to your instructor's requirements. (If no requirements are specified, follow the guidelines given in Appendix A.)

The key to producing a clean final draft is down time—an interim in which you leave the last draft alone and focus on something else. Coming back to your paper after a day or so away from it can help you see errors that passed right by you before. You may be surprised how many mistakes this fresh look can reveal. If you cannot set the essay aside, ask a friend to read it and give you some constructive criticism.

QUICK REVIEW: Steps in Writing a Philosophy Paper

Step 1: Select a topic and narrow it to a specific issue.

Step 2: Research the issue.

Step 3: Write a thesis statement.

Step 4: Create an outline of the whole essay.

Step 5: Write a first draft.

Step 6: Study and revise your first draft.

Step 7: Produce a final draft.

AN ANNOTATED SAMPLE PAPER

The following is the full version of the divine command essay, which demonstrates many of the considerations discussed in this chapter—organization, argument, thesis, explanation, sentence clarity, and more.

The Divine Command Theory

1 Many people believe that God is a lawgiver who alone defines what actions are right and wrong. God, in other words, is the author of morality; an action is right if and only if God commands it to be done. According to this view, there is no right or wrong until God says so, and nothing is moral or immoral independently of God's willing it to be thus. God, and only God, *makes* rightness and wrongness. This view is known as the divine command theory of morality.

Introduces topic.

Defines key term.

2 A simple version of the theory is widely accepted today, among both the religious and nonreligious. In this version, God is thought to be the source of all moral principles and values. He can be the source of all morality because he is omnipotent, being able to do anything whatsoever, including create the very foundations of right and wrong.

Specifies the version of the theory to be discussed.

Source is cited.

3 In the *Euthyphro*, Socrates brings out what is probably the oldest and strongest criticism of the theory. He asks, in effect, is an action right because God commands it to be done, or does God command it to be done because it is right?[1] This question lays bare the dilemma that is inherent in the theory: If an action is right because God commands it, then there is nothing in the action itself that makes it right, and God's command is arbitrary. If God commands the action because it is right (that is, he does not *make* it right), then rightness would seem to be independent of (or prior to) God, and the divine command theory is false. I contend that, at

Provides further background on issue.

2

least in the simplest version of the theory, this ancient dilemma still stands and that the most plausible way to resolve it is to reject the theory by accepting that moral standards must exist independently of God's commands.

Thesis statement.

4 The central argument against the notion that rightness is whatever God commands is this: If an action is right only because God commands it (that is, nothing is right or wrong in itself, or independent of God), then cruelty, murder, torture, and many other terrible actions would be right if God commanded them. If God commanded such acts, then they would be right, and no one would be committing a wrong by doing them. On the simple version of the theory, there are no limits whatsoever to God's power, so he could indeed command such things. If nothing would be right or wrong until God wills it, he could have no reason to either command murder or forbid it, to sanction the torture of innocents or prohibit it. Therefore, if God commands rightness, God's commands would be arbitrary—a result that would be implausible to the religious and nonreligious alike.

Writer presents first argument for thesis.

5 A parallel argument is also possible. As stated above, if an action is right only because God commands it, then cruelty, murder, torture, and many other terrible actions would be right if God commanded them. This means that such immoral actions—immoral in light of common moral standards—could be transformed by God into moral actions. This

Writer presents second argument for thesis.

3

outcome, however, would also be implausible to both the religious and nonreligious.

6 The main objection to the above arguments is that God would never command us to commit heinous acts. He would not because he is morally perfect—all-good in all ways. This counterargument, however, begs the question; it is a circular argument. The divine command theory is offered to explain what makes an action right—what makes something morally good. But to try to define what good is by saying that God is good is to talk in a circle: God's commands are good, and they are good because they are God's commands. This definition reduces the divine command theory to empty doubletalk. If we wish to have a better understanding of what makes an action right, we cannot be satisfied with such a definition.

Writer explains and rebuts main objection to thesis.

7 Moral philosopher James Rachels makes this same argument in a slightly different way:

Quotation is introduced.

8 [If] we accept the idea that good and bad are defined by reference to God's will, this notion is deprived of any meaning. What could it mean to say that God's commands are good? If "X is good" means "X is commanded by God," then "God's commands are good" would mean only "God's commands are commanded by God," an empty truism.[2]

Quote from source, with endnote.

4

9 To return to Socrates' dilemma, either an action is right only because God commands it, or an action is right (or wrong) independently of God's commands. As we have seen, if an action is right only because God commands it, then God's commands must be arbitrary, and it is possible for him to sanction obviously immoral acts. Since both these consequences are unacceptable, we must accept the second alternative: Rightness must be independent of (or prior to) God's commands. We therefore must reject the simplest version of the divine command theory.

Conclusion.

Summary of arguments for thesis and thesis restatement.

---

[1]Plato, *Euthyphro* in *The Trial and Death of Socrates* (Cambridge: Hackett, 1975).
[2]James Rachels, *The Elements of Moral Philosophy* (New York: McGraw-Hill Higher Education, 2003), 51.

⊰ 5 ⊱

Avoiding Fallacious Reasoning

As you surely must know by now, arguments are the main focus of most philosophical writing. Recall that an argument is a combination of statements in which some of them are intended to support another one of them. The statement meant to be supported is the conclusion; the statements meant to do the supporting are the premises. The premises are supposed to be the reasons for accepting the conclusion. As a reader of philosophy, you want to determine whether the arguments you encounter are good ones. As a writer of philosophy, you want to ensure that the arguments you use to make your case are also good. You want to avoid being fooled by, or fooling others with, a bad argument.

You can become more proficient in these skills if you know how to identify fallacies when you see them. *Fallacies* are common but bad arguments. They are defective arguments that appear so often in writing and speech that philosophers have given them names and offered instructions on how to recognize and avoid them.

Many fallacies are not just failed arguments—they are also deceptively plausible appeals. They can easily appear sound or cogent, misleading both you and your readers. Their potential for slipperiness is another good reason to study fallacies.

This chapter reviews many of the most common fallacies, explaining why they are bogus and how to detect them in your everyday reading and writing. The best way to use this material is to study each fallacy until you can consistently pick it out of any random selection of prose.

STRAW MAN

The *straw man* fallacy is the misrepresentation of a person's views so he or she can be more easily attacked or dismissed. Let's say you argue that the war in Iraq is too costly in lives and money, and your opponent replies this way:

> My adversary argues that the war in Iraq is much too difficult for the United States and that we ought to, in effect, cut and run while we can. But why must we take the coward's way out?

Thus, your point has been distorted, made to look more extreme or radical than it really is; it is now an easy target. The notion that we ought to "cut and run" or "take the coward's way out" *does not follow* from the statement that the war in Iraq is too costly.

The straw man kind of distortion, of course, proves nothing, although many people fall for it everyday. This fallacy is probably the most common type of fallacious reasoning used in politics. It is also popular in many other kinds of argumentation—including student philosophy papers.

APPEAL TO THE PERSON

Closely related to the straw man fallacy is *appeal to the person* (also known as the *ad hominem* fallacy). Appeal to the person is the rejecting of a statement on the grounds that it comes from a particular person, not because the statement, or claim, itself is false or dubious. For example:

> You can safely discard anything that Susan has to say about government. She's a dyed-in-the-wool socialist.

> Johnson argues that our current welfare system is defective. But don't listen to him—he's a conservative.

Each of these arguments is defective because it asks us to reject a claim because of a person's character, background, or circumstances—things that are generally irrelevant to the truth of claims. A statement must stand or fall *on its own merits*. The personal characteristics of the person espousing the view do not necessarily have a bearing on its truth. Only if we can show that someone's dubious traits somehow make the claim dubious are we justified in rejecting the claim because of a person's personal characteristics. Such a circumstance is rare.

Ad Hominem Attacks in Your Paper

Ad hominem arguments often creep into student philosophy papers. Part of the reason is that some appeals to the person are not so obvious. For example:

- "Swinburne's cosmological argument is a serious attempt to show that God is the best explanation for the existence of the universe. However, he is a well-known theist, and this fact raises some doubts about the strength of his case."

- "Dennett argues from the materialist standpoint, so he begins with a bias that we need to take into account."

- "Some of the strongest arguments against the death penalty come from a few people who are actually on death row. They obviously have a vested interest in showing that capital punishment is morally wrong. We therefore are forced to take their arguments—however convincing—with a grain of salt."

APPEAL TO POPULARITY

Appeal to popularity (or *appeal to the masses*) is another extremely common fallacy. It is arguing that a claim must be true not because it is backed by good reasons but simply because many people believe it. The idea is that, somehow, there is truth in numbers. For example:

Of course there's a God. Everyone believes that.

Seventy percent of Americans believe that the president's tax cuts are good for the economy. So don't try to tell me the tax cuts aren't good for the economy.

Most people believe that Jones is guilty, so he's guilty.

In each of these arguments, the conclusion is thought to be true merely because it is believed by an impressive number of people. The number of people who believe a claim, however, is irrelevant to the claim's truth. What really matters is how much support the claim has from good reasons. Large groups of people have been—and are—

wrong about many things. Many people once believed that Earth is flat, mermaids are real, and human sacrifices help crops grow. They were wrong.

Remember, however, that the number of people who accept a claim *can* be relevant to its truth if the people happen to be experts. Twenty professional astronomers who predict an eclipse are more reliable than one hundred nonexperts who swear that no such eclipse will occur.

APPEAL TO TRADITION

Appeal to tradition is actually a kind of appeal to popularity. It is arguing that merely because a claim is sanctioned by tradition, it must be true. This kind of argument says, in effect, that a statement is true because it has been held (or approved of) for a long time. Appeal to tradition is fallacious because the longevity of a traditional claim is logically irrelevant to its truth. Claims backed by a long tradition can be wrong—and often are. Consider:

> The death penalty is a just punishment for heinous crimes. This view has been the traditional stand that this community has always taken. There can be no doubt about it.

> Ancient shaman medicine works. Native Americans have used it for hundreds of years.

On the other hand, dismissing a claim just because it is traditional is also fallacious. The mere fact that a claim is traditional is no good reason for rejecting it. Rejection or acceptance must be based on adequate grounds.

GENETIC FALLACY

A ploy like appeal to the person is the *genetic fallacy*—arguing that a statement can be judged true or false based on its source. In appeal to the person, someone's character or circumstances is thought to tell the tale. In the genetic fallacy, the truth of a statement is supposed to depend on origins other than an individual—organizations, political platforms, groups, schools of thought, even exceptional states of mind (like dreams and intuitions). Look:

> That new military reform idea has gotta be bunk. It comes from a liberal think tank.

At the city council meeting Hernando said that he had a plan to curb the number of car crashes on highway 19. But you can bet that whatever it is, it's half-baked—he said the plan came to him when he was stoned on marijuana.

The U.S. Senate is considering a proposal to reform affirmative action, but you know their ideas must be ridiculous. What do they know about the rights of the disadvantaged? They're a bunch of rich, white guys.

EQUIVOCATION

The fallacy of *equivocation* is assigning two different meanings to the same significant word in an argument. The word is used in one sense in a premise and in a different sense in another place in the argument. The switch in meaning can deceive the reader and disrupt the argument, rendering it invalid or weaker than it would be otherwise. Here's a classic example:

Only man is rational.
No woman is a man.
Therefore, no woman is rational.

And one other:

You are a bad writer.
If you are a bad writer, then you are a bad boy.
Therefore, you are a bad boy.

The first argument equivocates on the word *man*. In the first premise, *man* means humankind; in the second, male. Thus, the argument seems to prove that women are not rational. You can see the trick better if you assign the same meaning to both instances of *man*. Like this:

Only humans are rational.
No woman is a human.
Therefore, no woman is rational.

In the second argument, the equivocal term is *bad*. In the first premise, *bad* means incompetent; in the second, immoral.

APPEAL TO IGNORANCE

As its name implies, this fallacy tries to prove something by appealing to what we *don't* know. *Appeal to ignorance* is arguing either that (1) a claim is true because it hasn't been proven false or (2) a claim is false because it hasn't been proven true. For example:

Try as they may, scientists have never been able to disprove the existence of an afterlife. The conclusion to be drawn from this is that there is in fact an afterlife.

Super Green Algae can cure cancer. No scientific study has ever shown that it does not work.

No one has ever shown that ESP (extrasensory perception) is real. Therefore, it does not exist.

There is no evidence that people on welfare are hardworking and responsible. Therefore, they are not hardworking and responsible.

The first two arguments try to prove a claim by pointing out that it hasn't been proven false. The second two try to prove that a claim is false because it hasn't been proven true. Both kinds of arguments are bogus because they assume that a lack of evidence proves something. A lack of evidence, however, can prove nothing. Being ignorant of the facts does not enlighten us.

Notice that if a lack of evidence could prove something, then you could prove just about anything you wanted. You could reason, for instance, that since no one can prove that horses *can't* fly, horses must be able to fly. Since no can disprove that you possess supernatural powers, you must possess supernatural powers.

Appeal to ignorance often takes the form of asking someone to prove a universal negative. A universal negative is a claim that nothing of a particular kind exists. Can you prove that flying horses don't exist? Can you prove that purple gremlins don't exist? How about unicorns or centaurs? Such requests for proof are utterly unreasonable because they ask the impossible. To prove that flying horses or unicorns don't exist, you would have to do something that no one can do—search all space and time. You can, of course, prove a more limited negative claim, such as "There are no books in this house" or "There are no fish in this pond." Requests for proof of a universal negative, however, are both absurd and unfair.

FALSE DILEMMA

In a dilemma, you are forced to choose between two unattractive possibilities. The fallacy of *false dilemma* is arguing erroneously that since there are only two alternatives to choose from, and one of them is unacceptable, the other one must be true. Consider these:

> You have to listen to reason. Either you must sell your car to pay your rent, or your landlord will throw you out on the street. You obviously aren't going to sell your car, so you will be evicted.

> You have to face the hard facts about the war on drugs. Either we must spend billions of dollars to increase military and law enforcement operations against drug cartels, or we must legalize all drugs. We obviously are not going to legalize all drugs, so we have to spend billions on anti-cartel operations.

The first argument says that there are only two choices to consider: either sell your car or get evicted, and since you will not sell your car, you will get evicted. This argument is fallacious because (presumably) the first premise is false—there seem to be more than just two alternatives here. You could get a job, borrow money from a friend, or sell your DVD player and TV. If the argument seems convincing, it is because other possibilities are excluded.

The second argument asserts that there are only two ways to go: spend billions to attack drug cartels or legalize all drugs. Since we won't legalize all drugs, we must therefore spend billions to assault the cartels. The first (either/or) premise, however, is false; there are at least three other options. The billions could be spent to reduce and prevent drug use, drug producers could be given monetary incentives to switch to nondrug businesses, or only some drugs could be legalized.

BEGGING THE QUESTION

The fallacy of *begging the question* is trying to prove a conclusion by using that very same conclusion as support. It is arguing in a circle. This way of trying to prove something says, in effect, "X is true because X is true." Few people would fall for this fallacy in such a simple form, but more subtle kinds can be beguiling. For example, here's the classic instance of begging the question, a staple of critical thinking textbooks:

> The Bible says that God exists.
>
> The Bible is true because God wrote it.
>
> Therefore, God exists.

The conclusion here ("God exists") is supported by premises that assume that very conclusion.

Here's another one:

> All citizens have the right to a fair trial because those whom the state is obliged to protect and give consideration are automatically due judicial criminal proceedings that are equitable by any reasonable standard.

This passage may at first seem like a good argument, but it isn't. It reduces to this unimpressive assertion: "All citizens have the right to a fair trial because all citizens have the right to a fair trial." The conclusion is "All citizens have the right to a fair trial," but that's more or less what the premise says. The premise—"those whom the state is obliged to protect and give consideration are automatically due judicial criminal proceedings that are equitable by any reasonable standard"—is equivalent to "All citizens have the right to a fair trial."

When circular reasoning is subtle, it can ensnare even its own creators. The fallacy can easily sneak into an argument if the premise and conclusion say the same thing but say it in different, complicated ways.

HASTY GENERALIZATION

The fallacy of *hasty generalization* is drawing a conclusion about a whole group, or class, of things based on an inadequate sample of the group. For example:

> All three of the college professors I've met in my lifetime were bald. Therefore, all college professors are bald.

> I interviewed over one hundred students at UC Berkeley, and eighty of them were Democrats. Therefore, 80 percent of all college students are Democrats.

For a whole week, I stood outside the art museum and interviewed people entering or leaving the building. I asked them if they listened to National Public Radio, and 70 percent said that they did. Obviously, most of the people in this city listen to National Public Radio.

A sample can be inadequate because it is too small or not representative enough. In the first argument, the sample is ridiculously inadequate. The most obvious problem, of course, is that the sample is much too small (it is also unrepresentative). You can draw no reliable conclusions about all college professors based on a sample of three.

The sample in the second argument is also inadequate. No matter how large the sample is at Berkeley, it will not be representative of all college students. With their views ranging across the political spectrum, college students are a politically diverse bunch. The views of Berkeley students are likely to differ from those of students at many other colleges.

The sample in the third argument suffers from the same problem. Since the survey was conducted in front of an art museum, the sample is likely to reflect the preferences of museum patrons, not of the whole city. The sample, whether large or small, will not be representative enough.

SLIPPERY SLOPE

The metaphor behind this fallacy suggests the danger of stepping on a precarious incline, losing your footing, and sliding to disaster. The fallacy of *slippery slope*, then, is arguing erroneously that a particular action should not be taken because it will lead inevitably to other actions resulting in some dire outcome. The key word here is *erroneously*. A slippery slope scenario becomes fallacious when there is no reason to believe that the chain of events predicted will ever happen. For example:

> This trend toward gay marriage must be stopped. If gay marriage is permitted, then traditional marriage between a man and a woman will be debased and devalued, which will lead to an increase in divorces. And higher divorce rates can only harm our children.

This argument is fallacious because there are no reasons for believing that gay marriage will ultimately result in the chain of events described. If good reasons could be given, the argument might be salvaged.

COMPOSITION

Sometimes what is true about the parts of a thing is also true of the whole—and sometimes not. The fallacy of *composition* is arguing erroneously that what can be said of the parts can also be said of the whole. Consider:

Each piece of wood that makes up this house is lightweight. Therefore, the whole house is lightweight.

Each soldier in the platoon is proficient. Therefore the platoon as a whole is proficient.

The monthly payments on this car are low. Hence, the cost of the car is low.

Just remember, sometimes the whole does have the same properties as the parts. If each part of the rocket is made of steel, the whole rocket is made of steel.

DIVISION

If you turn the fallacy of composition upside down, you get the fallacy of *division*—arguing erroneously that what can be said of the whole can be said of the parts:

The house is heavy. Therefore, every part of the house is heavy.

The platoon is very effective. Therefore, every member of the platoon is effective.

That herd of elephants eats an enormous amount of food each day. Therefore, each elephant in the herd eats an enormous amount of food each day.

QUICK REVIEW: Common Fallacies

- *Straw Man:* The misrepresentation of a person's views so he or she can be more easily attacked or dismissed.

- *Appeal to the Person:* Rejecting a statement on the grounds that it comes from a particular person, not because the statement, or claim, itself is false or dubious.

- *Appeal to Popularity:* Arguing that a claim must be true not because it is backed by good reasons but simply because many people believe it.

- *Appeal to Tradition:* Arguing that merely because a claim is sanctioned by tradition, it must be true.

- *Genetic Fallacy:* Arguing that a statement can be judged true or false based on its source.

- *Equivocation:* Assigning two different meanings to the same word in an argument.

- *Appeal to Ignorance:* Arguing either that (1) a claim is true because it hasn't been proven false or (2) a claim is false because it hasn't been proven true.

- *False Dilemma:* Arguing erroneously that since there are only two alternatives to choose from, and one of them is unacceptable, the other one must be true.

- *Begging the Question:* Trying to prove a conclusion by using that very same conclusion as support.

- *Hasty Generalization:* Drawing a conclusion about a whole group, or class, of things based on an inadequate sample of the group.

- *Slippery Slope:* Arguing erroneously that a particular action should not be taken because it will lead inevitably to other actions resulting in some dire outcome.

- *Composition:* Arguing erroneously that what can be said of the parts can be said of the whole.

- *Division:* Arguing erroneously that what can be said of the whole can be said of the parts.

⇥ 6 ⇤

Using, Quoting, and Citing Sources

Probably very few philosophy papers are written without relying at some point and in some way on other writings—essays, books, journals, magazines, and reference works. Reliance on such sources generally makes for better philosophy papers. The problem is, many writers do not know how to use sources properly and productively, and their papers (and grades) suffer accordingly. If you fit this category, the following rules should help you now and serve as a useful reference later on.

Rule 6-1 Know When and How to Quote Sources

To quote something is to use someone's exact words in your own writing. If you decide to quote, you should do so only for good reasons. One good reason is that the author's words are the clearest or best expression of a point you want to make (otherwise a paraphrase or summary may be more effective). Another reason is that you are criticizing or explaining the author's claim or argument and it is important to show precisely how the author expresses it. In general, you should not use quotations for reasons *unrelated* to your paper's thesis. For example, you should not quote just because you cannot think of anything to say, because you want to disguise your lack of understanding of the material, or because you want to stretch your paper to the required length. Your instructor will see through these tactics. Worse, they will probably add to your ignorance of the subject matter.

Quotations are not like seasoning; they cannot be sprinkled randomly throughout your paper to improve its overall flavor. Every quotation must be properly introduced and explained. When you quote material, you must ensure that your reader knows who wrote it (you or someone else) and how it is related to your thesis as well as the point at hand. Your reader should never have to think, "Whose words are these, and what do they have to do with this discussion?"

Here are some examples of common ways to incorporate quotations into your paper:

> Even if there is an evil genius, Descartes believes that there is at least one thing that he knows, namely, that he exists. "Then without doubt I exist also if he deceives me," Descartes says, "and let him deceive me as much as he will, he can never cause me to be nothing so long as I think that I am something."[1]

> This argument starts from a fact about the world and then tries to show that the existence of God is the best explanation of that fact. Richard Gale, however, sums up the deep-seated problem with such an argument: "The most telling objection that can be lodged against the cosmological argument is that it is impossible for such a being to exist, thereby showing that this argument's conclusion is necessarily false."[2]

> This argument starts from a fact about the world and then tries to show that the existence of God is the best explanation of that fact. Richard Gale, however, points out that the most serious objection that can be raised against the God of the cosmological argument is that "it is impossible for such a being to exist, thereby showing that this argument's conclusion is necessarily false."[3]

Notice that to signal the beginning and ending of the words of a quotation, you insert quotation marks before and after them. Except in a few cases noted later in this chapter, none other than the author's precise wording is allowed between the quotation marks—no paraphrase, no summary, no added words.

Very long quotations are set off without quotation marks in what is known as block form. Customarily, quotations of four to ten manuscript lines are put in block form. Block quotes are usually

---

[1]René Descartes, *Meditation II*, trans. Elizabeth Haldane and G. R. T. Ross, in *The Philosophical Works of Descartes*, vol. 1 (Cambridge: Cambridge University Press, 1931), 150.
[2]Richard M. Gale, *On the Nature and Existence of God* (Cambridge: Cambridge University Press, 1991), 238–39.
[3]Gale, 238–39.

separated from regular text by leaving extra space above and below the block quote and by indenting the left edge of the block quote. For example:

> If a prediction turns out to be false, we can always save the hypothesis by modifying the background theory. As Philip Kitcher notes:
>
>> Individual scientific claims do not, and cannot, confront the evidence one by one. Rather . . . "hypotheses are tested in bundles.". . . We can only test relatively large bundles of claims. What this means is that when our experiments go awry we are not logically compelled to select any particular claim as the culprit. We can always save a cherished hypothesis from refutation by rejecting (however implausibly) one of the other members of the bundle.[4]

As mentioned earlier, direct quotations should match the original passage word for word. The corollary to this rule is that you may alter quotations (1) if the change does not distort the author's meaning and (2) if the change is properly signaled to the reader. Writers sometimes alter quotations to make them easier to read or to eliminate extraneous material.

One way to indicate that a quotation has been altered is to use ellipsis marks—three consecutive dots, or periods, with a space before and after each one. You use ellipsis marks to show that words have been omitted from a quotation. Use them to indicate an omission inside a sentence.

> William Frankena argues that any adequate moral theory must incorporate some principle of justice but that the principle must not be too broad. As he points out, "Treating people equally . . . does not mean making their lives equally good or maintaining their lives at the same level of goodness."[5]

Here, the words "in this sense" have been omitted; they are unnecessary because the intended sense has already been established.

Also use ellipsis marks to show that a whole sentence or more has been omitted. If the omitted material comes after a complete sentence, insert the ellipsis dots after that sentence's period.

> Utilitarianism does not require that only the guilty be punished or that the punishment fit the crime. The categorical imperative, however,

---

[4]Philip Kitcher, "Believing Where We Cannot Prove," in *Abusing Science* (Cambridge: MIT Press, 1982), 44.

[5]William K. Frankena, *Ethics*, 2nd ed. (Englewood Cliffs: Prentice-Hall, 1973), 51.

requires both. As Kant says:

> But what is the mode and measure of punishment which public justice takes as its principle and standard? It is just the principle of equality, by which the pointer of the scale of justice is made to incline more to the one side than to the other. . . . Hence it may be said: "If you slander another, you slander yourself; if you steal from another, you steal from yourself; if you strike another, you strike yourself; if you kill another, you kill yourself." This is the only principle which . . . can definitely assign both the quality and the quantity of a just penalty.[6]

Another way to signal that a quotation has been changed is to use brackets (also known as square brackets): [ ]. You use brackets to add or substitute your own words into a quotation to clarify wording or to make the quotation's grammar fit into the surrounding text.

> By questioning the control exercised by autonomous man and demonstrating the control of the environment, a science of behavior also seems to question [human] dignity and worth. [The traditional view is that a] person is responsible for his behavior, not only in the sense that he may be justly punished when he behaves badly, but also in the sense that he is to be given credit and admired for his achievements. A scientific analysis shifts the credit as well as the blame to the environment, and traditional practices can then no longer be justified.[7]

Remember, whether you use ellipsis marks or brackets, you must be sure *not* to misrepresent the author's meaning.

Rule 6-2 Do Not Plagiarize

Plagiarism is theft of someone else's ideas or words, whether deliberate or accidental. (Most is accidental.) Plagiarism is a serious offense against readers, the author whose work is stolen, and the ideal of academic integrity. There are both academic and legal penalties for plagiarism, and these are usually extremely harsh.

You steal another's ideas or words when you use them in your own work without acknowledging their true source. You commit plagiarism when:

1. You do not make clear exactly what you borrow from a source.
2. You do not make clear exactly who the source is of what you borrow.

---

[6]Immanuel Kant, *The Metaphysical Elements of Justice*, trans. John Ladd (Indianapolis: Bobbs-Merrill, 1965), 99–107.

[7]B. F. Skinner, *Beyond Freedom and Dignity* (New York: Bantam, 1971), 17, 19.

You violate guideline 1 if (a) you do not enclose verbatim repetition of someone else's wording in quotation marks or (b) you do not plainly distinguish between your own ideas, opinions, and arguments and those of others. You violate guideline 2 if you do not properly cite the source of the material you use.

Using another writer's exact words without enclosing them in quotation marks is the most blatant form of plagiarism. It is a clear-cut violation of guideline 1. You are, however, also guilty of plagiarism if you do not acknowledge, or cite, the author of an exact quote—whether or not it is flagged with quotation marks. This error is a violation of guideline 2.

Likewise, you are guilty of plagiarism if you paraphrase or summarize another writer's work without properly citing it. When you paraphrase or summarize, you are not quoting directly, but you are presenting the author's ideas, opinions, or arguments. If you don't acknowledge the author as the source, you are representing the ideas, opinions, or arguments as your own—a violation of guideline 2. You are also guilty of plagiarism if you paraphrase or summarize an author's work, acknowledge the source, but fail to accurately distinguish between the author's ideas and your own—a violation of guideline 1.

Plagiarism refers to the unacknowledged use of someone else's work. It does not, however, apply to material that is considered common knowledge—that is, facts that are generally well known or well known among experts in a particular field. There is no sense, for example, in citing anyone as the source of the fact that Immanuel Kant died in 1804, that water freezes at 32° F, that a bird in hand is worth two in the bush, or that *modus ponens* is a valid argument form.

Determining what is common knowledge in a particular field can be a challenge for those who are new to a discipline. In general, if you come across the same facts frequently in an area of study or if they are commonplace information in reference works, you may assume that they are common knowledge. If you aren't sure what you should or should not cite, ask your instructor.

To sum up, plagiarism can take any one of these forms:

- Quoting the author directly without including *both* quotation marks and a citation.

- Paraphrasing or summarizing an argument without citing the source.

- Including in paraphrases or summaries some of the author's exact wording without putting it in quotation marks.

- Imitating too closely the author's language and style in paraphrases and summaries (a violation even when you cite the source).

Rule 6-3   Cite Your Sources Carefully

When you cite sources in your paper, you should use a citation, or documentation, system that indicates precisely who or what your sources are. There are several systems available, and your instructor may require you to use a particular one. Two of them, however, enjoy considerable currency in the humanities, and we will closely examine both of them here.

The *documentary-note* (or *humanities*) *system* is the documentation scheme used most in philosophy. This system is given its most detailed and authoritative description in *The Chicago Manual of Style* (CMS).[8] It features superscript (small, raised) numbers in the text that refer to information in footnotes (at the bottom of the page) or in endnotes (at the end of the paper). Instructors often insist that it be accompanied by a bibliography (Rule 6-4).

The other approach is the *author-page system,* a form of which is recommended by the Modern Language Association (MLA).[9] It provides some source information in the text itself (for example, author's name and page number) and further, corresponding information in an end-of-paper list usually called "Works Cited" or "References." The text citation may consist of both the author's name and the page number in parentheses, or the author's name mentioned in a sentence of the text with the page number nearby in parentheses.

Appendix B explains how to document sources using either the CMS documentary-note or the MLA author-page system. You can find more information about these in the CMS and MLA publications.

Rule 6-4   Build a Bibliography if Needed

A bibliography is a list of sources used in researching and writing a paper. Often instructors ask students to include a bibliography in

---

[8]*The Chicago Manual of Style,* 15th ed. (Chicago: University of Chicago Press, 2003).
[9]*MLA Handbook for Writers of Research Papers,* 6th ed. (New York: MLA, 2003).

papers—even if the papers already have pages of notes. They are less likely to ask for a bibliography in a paper using the author-page system of documentation, however, because the list of works cited can take the place of a bibliography. In any case, the final word on whether to include a bibliography must come from your instructor.

A bibliography must include all works cited in the paper, but sometimes it also contains sources consulted but not cited. This is another point that your instructor can clarify.

You should alphabetize a bibliography by the last names of authors or editors or, if the author is unknown, by the first significant word of the title of the work (that is, excluding the words *the*, *an*, and *a*). The bibliography should appear after reference notes, starting on a new page. It should also be paginated along with the rest of the paper.

Treat entries as you would a list of works cited (in the MLA documentation system): the first line of an entry is flush left, and subsequent lines are indented. If there are several works written by the same author, the first one includes the author's name, but the ones that follow replace the name with three hyphens and a period.

As it turns out, the basic format of the MLA list of works cited is almost identical to that of the bibliography suggested by the CMS. To simplify matters, you can use the works-cited guidelines to create a bibliography for a paper using the CMS documentary-note system. Determine if your instructor has a preference. Whatever the case, the CMS and the *MLA Handbook* can provide authoritative help.

⊰ PART 2 ⊱

REFERENCE GUIDE

The following two chapters constitute a brief catalog of rules for good writing—a quick reference to many of the most common errors and essential skills. Chapter 7 covers the crafting of effective sentences; Chapter 8, the basics of word choice.

If you are serious about improving your writing, this guide should help you—whether you read it straight through from beginning to end or refer to it when you are confronted with a writing problem. If you want to use it as a reference, you can either page through the chapters or scan the book's extended index for a key word related to a particular writing error or skill. The index includes references to many writing skills, errors, and recommendations.

⚔ 7 ⚔

Writing Effective Sentences

Rule 7-1 Make the Subject and Verb Agree in Number and Person

A subject and verb must match up in number (singular or plural) and person (first, second, or third). If they do not agree, the sentence is not only grammatically incorrect but probably confusing and distracting as well.

CORRECT: The *clerk does* all the paperwork for you.
(The subject *clerk* is third person singular and agrees with the verb *does*.)

INCORRECT: The *clerk do* all the paperwork for you.
(The subject *clerk* is third person singular but does not agree with the verb *do*.)

Do not be confused by plural nouns that separate subject from verb. They do not alter the subject-verb relationship.

INCORRECT: The production of better trucks and of the many gadgets that make driving vehicles easier have changed the market.
(The subject is *production*, so the verb should be singular—*has changed*, not *have changed*.)

The indefinite pronouns *anyone, everyone, each, each one, someone, everybody, nobody, something, somebody, anything, neither,* and *either* take singular verbs.

INCORRECT: Every boy in the class are doing work.

CORRECT: Every boy in the class is doing work.

INCORRECT: Each of them are counting on you.

CORRECT: Each of them is counting on you.

INCORRECT: Nobody in the platoon shoot straight.

CORRECT: Nobody in the platoon shoots straight.

The indefinite pronouns *none* and *any*, however, take either a singular or plural verb depending on their reference. If they refer to a singular noun or pronoun, they require a singular verb; if a plural noun or pronoun, a plural verb. (Hint: Regard *none* as singular when it means "no one" or "not one.")

SINGULAR: None is exempt from prosecution.

PLURAL: None are repaired quickly enough.

Despite appearances to the contrary, a noun in the predicate does *not* determine the number of the verb. The subject determines the number.

INCORRECT: The biggest problem are all the trees that block the sun.

CORRECT: The biggest problem is the trees that block the sun.

BETTER: The trees that block the sun are the biggest problem.

INCORRECT: The tax hikes and the reduction in benefits is a disgrace.

CORRECT: The tax hikes and the reduction in benefits are a disgrace.

Consider sentences that have this form: ". . . one of the [plural noun] who [or that] + [verb] . . ." For example:

CORRECT: George is one of those guys who *work* hard.

The subject is *who*, and its antecedent is *guys*, not *one*. The verb *work*, therefore, must agree with *guys*.

In sentences of this form, the verb takes its number from the relative pronoun (*that* or *who*), which is plural because it refers to the plural noun preceding it. The exception to this tenet is that if *only* precedes *one*, the relative pronoun refers to one, not to the plural noun.

CORRECT: Maria is the only one of my friends who gets As in school.

In general, consider two or more subjects linked by *and* to be plural and therefore entitled to a plural verb.

CORRECT: The man's personal philosophy and his lack of income are at odds.

Sometimes two subjects linked by *and* actually refer to a single thing or the same thing. In such cases they should take a singular verb.

CORRECT: Ham and eggs is my favorite dish.

CORRECT: This old soldier and scout is a person of rare courage.

When a subject is singular, it stays singular even when it is coupled with other nouns by phrases such *as well as, along with, no less than, together with, accompanied by,* and *in addition to.*

CORRECT: Joshua as well as Fred and Susan is very cheerful.

CORRECT: The tide, along with the wind and the rain, was making the trip unbearable.

Rule 7-2   Express Parallel Ideas in Parallel Form

Parallelism is a fundamental principle of good writing. It says that similar ideas should be expressed in similar grammatical structures. Effective parallelism results in sentences that are both well balanced and readable. Lack of parallelism in places where it is needed can yield monstrous sentences and confused readers.

Problems often arise in sentences featuring a series of ideas linked by coordinating conjunctions such as *and, but,* and *or.*

NOT PARALLEL: In school you should strive for good grades, perfect attendance, and you should have friends.

PARALLEL: In school you should strive for good grades, perfect attendance, and generous friends.

This series consists of three similar ideas, but its structure is not parallel. It starts with a couple of nouns and ends with a clause. The remedy is to make all three items in the series either nouns or clauses.

NOT PARALLEL: Juan's goals are to finish high school, to graduate from college, and a job.

PARALLEL: Juan's goals are to finish high school, to graduate from college, and to get a job.

Again we have three similar ideas encased in a nonparallel structure. The first two items in the series are infinitive phrases, but the final one is a noun. Ensuring that all three items are infinitive phrases fixes the problem.

NOT PARALLEL: I will serve for duty, for honor, and country.

PARALLEL: I will serve for duty, for honor, and for country.

Paired ideas should also be put in similar form.

NOT PARALLEL: I see that you are both thrifty and are practical.

PARALLEL: I see that you are both thrifty and practical.

NOT PARALLEL: She is neither a scholar with distinction nor is she a dabbler with curiosity.

PARALLEL: She is neither a scholar with distinction nor a dabbler with curiosity.

NOT PARALLEL: Being lost in the jungle is better than the prospects of the tribe eating us in the village.

PARALLEL: Being lost in the jungle is better than being eaten in the village.

Rule 7-3   Write in Complete Sentences, Not Fragments

A sentence is a group of words that comprise a subject and verb and that can stand alone (that is, function as an independent clause). A sentence fragment is a group of words that looks like a sentence but is, in fact, merely part of a sentence. Here are a few fragments ensconced with some complete sentences (the fragments are underlined).

FRAGMENT: I decided to ride my bicycle into town. Because my car was out of gas.

FRAGMENT: Jane says she will never go to another football game. Although many of her friends think that she likes the game.

FRAGMENT: The government may be fooling us with dirty tricks. Such as pretending to care about taxpayers while plotting to raise taxes.

FRAGMENT: I was able to do a lot of research at the library. <u>Going through just about every journal in the field</u>.

You can get rid of a fragment in your writing by (1) deleting it (the most obvious solution), (2) attaching it to a complete sentence, or (3) turning it into a complete sentence. For example:

FRAGMENT: The government may be fooling us with dirty tricks. Such as pretending to care about taxpayers while plotting to raise taxes.

ATTACHED TO A SENTENCE: The government may be fooling us with dirty tricks, pretending to care about taxpayers while plotting to raise taxes.

TURNED INTO A SENTENCE: The government may be fooling us with dirty tricks. It may be pretending to care about taxpayers while plotting to raise taxes.

From time to time, even the best writers use fragments. They use them sparingly, however, and only for good reasons (such as to add emphasis). Inexperienced writers should avoid using fragments in their academic writing—unless they too have good reasons (which is usually not the case).

Rule 7-4   Connect Independent Clauses Properly

Sometimes inexperienced writers jam two independent clauses together without connecting them correctly. The result is a run-on sentence.

RUN-ON: Rosa cleaned the office from top to bottom she was finished by the end of the day.

RUN-ON: Politicians never seem to tell the truth, how can they live with themselves?

RUN-ON: I knew Aziz was there, I could see his head half-hidden by the curtain.

The first example is a kind of run-on called a fused sentence. It forces two independent clauses together without any punctuation or connecting word at all. The other two examples are called comma splices because the clauses are joined by just a comma when a much stronger or clearer connection is required. You can easily mend all of these depending on what meaning you want to convey.

You can repair the fused sentence by joining the two clauses with *both* a comma and a coordinating conjunction (*and, or, but, for, yet, so*). The comma always goes in front of the conjunction.

REPAIRED: Rosa cleaned the office from top to bottom, and she was finished by the end of the day.

You can achieve a similar effect by joining the clauses with a semicolon. In this kind of construction, no coordinating conjunction is necessary.

REPAIRED: Rosa cleaned the office from top to bottom; she was finished by the end of the day.

You can be more specific about the relationship between the two clauses by adding a conjunctive adverb such as *however, consequently,* and *therefore* after the semicolon.

REPAIRED: Rosa cleaned the office from top to bottom; therefore, she was finished by the end of the day.

In each of these revisions the two clauses are given more or less equal weight, with neither seeming to be more important than the other. Another approach, however, is to subordinate one of the clauses to the other.

REPAIRED: Because Rosa cleaned the office from top to bottom, she was finished by the end of the day.

Perhaps the most obvious option is to change the paired clauses into two distinct sentences.

REPAIRED: Rosa cleaned the office from top to bottom. She was finished by the end of the day.

You can modify the two comma splices, of course, in much the same way. The first one is composed of a declarative statement and a question, so the most plausible way to change it is to turn it into two sentences.

REPAIRED: Politicians never seem to tell the truth. How can they live with themselves?

At first you may consider correcting the second comma splice by adding a coordinating conjunction after the comma. You can achieve a more natural reading, however, by turning the clauses into separate sentences, joining them with a semicolon, or subordinating one of the clauses.

REPAIRED: I knew Aziz was there; I could see his head half-hidden by the curtain.

REPAIRED: I knew Aziz was there because I could see his head half-hidden by the curtain.

Rule 7-5   Delete the Deadwood

Wordiness is the use of more words than necessary to express your meaning. When you use twenty words to convey an idea that can be expressed easily in ten, you are being wordy. You are packing your writing with deadwood—needless words that merely fill space. Wordiness is measured not by how many words you use, but by how many *excess* words you use. Consider this passage:

> In light of the fact that an appreciable number of employed workers are exceeding their allotted allowance of excess working hours, it is necessary that for the time being excess hours must be suspended by the foreman until such time as the plant can be updated to better and more modern equipment.

Now compare it to this version:

> Because many employees are working too much overtime, the foreman must temporarily suspend it until we can modernize the plant.

These two sentences mean almost the same thing. The first one, however, uses fifty-two words to say it; the second one, twenty. The first is inefficient, hard to understand, stilted, and dull. The second one is far more concise, easier to grasp, and more vigorous. Readers would rather read a whole page of such economical writing than one paragraph of bloated, windy prose.

A common cause of wordiness is deadwood expressions—long phrases whose meaning could be stated in a mere word or two. All the following phrases have a concise substitute.

DEADWOOD	SUBSTITUTE
by means of	by
in a bold manner	boldly
in order to	to
due to the fact that	because
the reason why is that	because
have an effect upon	affect

DEADWOOD (*contd.*)	SUBSTITUTE (*contd.*)
in spite of the fact that	though, although
at the present time	now, currently
at this point in time	now, currently
he is a man who	he
she is a woman who	she
concerning the matter of	about, concerning
because of the fact that	because
until such time as	until
has the ability to	can
for the purpose of	to
in the event that	if
in terms of	for, in
give consideration to	consider
as to whether	whether
along the lines of	like

Rule 7-6   Put Modifiers in Their Place

Modifiers are words, phrases, or clauses that act as adjectives or adverbs. If you position modifiers incorrectly, confusion or hilarity may reign. If you place them properly, the reader will have no doubts about which word they modify, and your meaning will be clear.

In their writing, students often misplace modifying phrases and clauses. For example:

MISPLACED: Theo tried to change the tire while the rain was pouring down in a fit of rage.

IMPROVED: In a fit of rage, Theo tried to change the tire while the rain was pouring down.

The remedy here is to position the modifying phrase "in a fit of rage" closer to the word modified—Theo.

MISPLACED: He saw that the lights were off in the cabin while standing under a tree.

IMPROVED: While standing under a tree, he saw that the lights were off in the cabin.

Who or what was standing under a tree? The confusion is cleared up after moving "while standing under a tree" in front of "he."

MISPLACED: There is a flower in her apartment that smells like onions.

IMPROVED: In her apartment a flower smells like onions.

Relative clauses (like "that smells like onions") should usually follow immediately after their antecedents. *Flower* is the antecedent here, so the relative clause comes after it (although in this case the relative pronoun *that* is dropped).

When a modifier appears in a sentence without a word to modify, it is said to be dangling. Showing up often in student writing, dangling modifiers are sometimes hilarious and always either perplexing or distracting. Typically they appear as phrases at the start of a sentence and pretend to modify the word that immediately follows.

INCORRECT: Before shooting again, the squirrel fell near the hunter.

CORRECT: Before shooting again, the hunter watched the squirrel fall nearby.

INCORRECT: After loosening his tie and kicking off his shoes, the feather bed was the only thing Harry had on his mind.

CORRECT: After loosening his tie and kicking off his shoes, Harry could think only of the feather bed.

INCORRECT: To keep the students happy, the windows were opened.

CORRECT: To keep the students happy, we opened the windows.

Some words modify other words by restricting or limiting their meaning: for example, *only, even, nearly,* and *almost.* Unfortunately, when these adverbs are not inserted immediately before the words they modify, they become misplaced modifiers.

INCORRECT: I only learned of her illness yesterday.

CORRECT: I learned of her illness only yesterday.

INCORRECT: The government has determined that the rations should be only distributed to the neediest people.

CORRECT: The government has determined that the rations should be distributed only to the neediest people.

INCORRECT: I nearly spent all the money.

CORRECT: I spent nearly all the money.

Rule 7-7   Be Consistent in Tense, Voice, Number, and Person

If you begin writing with one grammatical structure then shift unnecessarily to another, you may confuse (or annoy) your reader. In sentences and paragraphs, you should stay with one tense, voice, number, and person unless you have a good reason for shifting.

SHIFTED: I walked past the front desk and into the stacks of the library. When I got to the philosophy section, I see a whole shelf of books about Kant. I stopped in my tracks.

This description of action begins in past tense then suddenly drops into present tense in the second sentence and back again to the past in the third. Making the tenses consistent throughout rectifies the problem.

CONSISTENT: I walked past the front desk and into the stacks of the library. When I got to the philosophy section, I saw a whole shelf of books about Kant. I stopped in my tracks.

In philosophical writing the convention is to discuss or summarize a philosopher's work in present tense. The events of a philosopher's life, however, are usually described in past tense.

CORRECT: In ordinary circumstances, however, the self seems to be unified, and any process theory must account for this apparent unity of the self. Immanuel Kant (1724–1804) accounts for it by postulating a "transcendental ego" that lies behind our experience and structures it according to certain rules. Kant's self is transcendental because it cannot be directly observed.[1]

You should also avoid unnecessary shifts in voice—from active to passive or passive to active. In active voice the subject does the action (*Maria spent the money*); in passive voice, the subject receives the action (*The money was spent by Maria*). Switching suddenly from

---

[1]Theodore Schick, Jr., and Lewis Vaughn, *Doing Philosophy: An Introduction Through Thought Experiments* (New York: McGraw-Hill, 2003), 277.

one to the other can be baffling or distracting to the reader. (See the discussion of active and passive voice in Rule 8-2.)

SHIFTED: I wrote the first half of my philosophy paper before I realized that the main argument was constructed poorly.

CONSISTENT: I wrote the first half of my philosophy paper before realizing that I had constructed the main argument poorly.

Careful writers ensure that pronouns and nouns are consistent in person (*I, you, he/she, we, you, they*) within a sentence or paragraph.

SHIFTED: Students must keep up with homework or you will fall behind in both your homework and tests.

This sentence begins in third person (*students*) but switches to second person (*you, your*) in the second clause. The solution is to stick with either third or second person throughout the sentence.

CONSISTENT: Students must keep up with homework, or they will fall behind in both homework and tests.

CONSISTENT: You must keep up with homework, or you will fall behind in both homework and tests.

Now consider this shift from first person to second.

SHIFTED: I was frightened as I walked past the graveyard because shadows can play tricks on your mind.

CONSISTENT: I was frightened as I walked past the graveyard because I knew that shadows can play tricks on my mind.

Rule 7-8 Communicate Pronoun References Clearly

Pronouns are supposed to refer to specific words—to nouns, the pronouns' antecedents. These references must be clear, or else readers will get sidetracked while trying to trace the path from pronoun to corresponding noun. The first rule of pronoun reference, then, is this: A pronoun should refer to particular words, not to a vague or general idea or to a word that is merely implied but not stated.

A common problem is the use of *this, that, which,* and *it* to refer not to a particular antecedent but to something more amorphous—a whole sentence or some blurry, unspoken notion.

VAGUE REFERENCE: Jill never entirely accepted the testimony of her own sister regarding the burglary. This is demonstrated in the way Jill refers to her sister's behavior.

To what does *This* refer? Here the reference is clear:

CLEAR REFERENCE: Jill never entirely accepted the testimony of her own sister regarding the burglary. This lack of acceptance is shown in the way Jill refers to her sister's behavior.

VAGUE REFERENCE: Descartes did not give in to overwhelming, all-encompassing doubt, which is why he was able to say, "I think therefore I am."

Which has no specific reference; it points—vaguely—to everything in the first clause.

CLEAR REFERENCE: Descartes did not give in to overwhelming, all-encompassing doubt. This refusal to doubt literally everything enabled him to say at least, "I think therefore I am."

VAGUE REFERENCE: In Frankena's *Ethics* it shows that moral theories have many subtypes.

CLEAR REFERENCE: In *Ethics* Frankena shows that moral theories have many subtypes.

Vague references using *they* are particularly prevalent but can be easily corrected.

VAGUE REFERENCE: They are trying to outlaw smoking in all bars, taverns, and clubs.

CLEAR REFERENCE: The state legislators are trying to outlaw smoking in all bars, taverns, and clubs.

Sometimes the reference of a pronoun is unclear because of ambiguity—the pronoun could refer to either of two antecedents.

AMBIGUOUS REFERENCE: Sharon was listening to the radio in her car when it suddenly stopped functioning.

CLEAR REFERENCE: Sharon was listening to the radio in her car when the engine suddenly stopped running.

AMBIGUOUS REFERENCE: Amelia just happened to mention to Eve that she was the wrong person for the job.

CLEAR REFERENCE: Amelia confided in Eve that she was not the right person for the job.

CLEAR REFERENCE: Amelia mentioned to Eve, "I am the wrong person for the job."

The antecedent of a pronoun must actually be contained in a sentence, not merely implied by the sentence's content.

IMPLIED REFERENCE: Thomas Aquinas's first-cause argument has some defects that he never recognized.

CLEAR REFERENCE: Thomas Aquinas never recognized the defects in his first-cause argument.

IMPLIED REFERENCE: After the airline disaster, I decided not to fly in one again.

CLEAR REFERENCE: After the airline disaster, I decided not to fly in a commercial jet again.

⚛ 8 ⚛

Choosing the Right Words

Rule 8-1 Select Nouns and Verbs Precisely

Sometimes writers are imprecise and wordy because they try to modify every noun and verb with an adjective or adverb. Carefully chosen nouns and verbs, however, often do not need to be modified. You need not write *walked slowly and clumsily* when *lumbered* will do, or *speak very softly* when *whispered* is fine, or *wrote hastily* when *jotted* is fitting. Likewise you have nothing to gain by writing *large house* if *mansion* will suffice, or *upper limb* when you mean *arm*.

Rule 8-2 Prefer the Active Voice

In active voice the subject does the action (*Kim drove the car*); in passive voice, the subject receives the action (*The car was driven by Kim*). Both constructions have their uses. Passive voice is appropriate when you want to focus on the receiver of the action or when the doer of the action cannot or should not be identified (for example, *The jewels were stolen last night*). In general, you should prefer the active voice in all other cases. Compared to passive voice, active voice is often more concise, more direct, and more vigorous.

> PASSIVE VOICE: Far to the west the mountainside was crashed into by the meteor.

> ACTIVE VOICE: Far to the west the meteor crashed into the mountainside.

PASSIVE VOICE: That all our knowledge is derived from experience was maintained by the empiricists—who are best represented by the British philosophers Locke, Berkeley, and Hume.

ACTIVE VOICE: The empiricists—who are best represented by the British philosophers Locke, Berkeley, and Hume—maintained that all our knowledge is derived from experience.

Rule 8-3   Use Specific Terms

General words refer to entire categories of things: *parent, vegetation, color, male, fast.* Specific words refer to more particular or definite examples of such categories: *Fran's mother, the grass on your lawn, that shade of red, John Smith, ninety miles per hour.* In some circumstances, a general word is best; in other instances, a more specific word. Good writers, however, strive to be as specific as a given context will allow. They know that specific terms often convey more information more vividly than general terms do.

GENERAL: She traveled back to her residence due to adverse weather.

SPECIFIC: Anne took a taxi back to her high-rise apartment because a snowstorm was pounding the city.

GENERAL: This moral theory forbids actions that can cause harm.

SPECIFIC: This moral theory, a consequentialist view, forbids actions that can cause physical pain to other people or put them at greater risk of experiencing physical pain.

Rule 8-4   Avoid Redundancy

A characteristic of writing that can increase wordiness and reduce clarity is redundancy—pointlessly expressing the same idea twice. Redundancy, which frequently arises in common phrases, suggests carelessness and ignorance of word meanings. Substitute concise terms for redundant ones.

REDUNDANT	NOT REDUNDANT
true facts	facts
refer back	refer
future forecast	forecast

REDUNDANT (contd.)	NOT REDUNDANT (contd.)
mix together	mix
few in number	few
absolute necessity	necessity
free gift	gift
collaborate together	collaborate
merge together	merge
advance planning	planning
connect together	connect

Rule 8-5   Be Aware of the Connotations of Words

A large part of making appropriate word choices is understanding the connotations of words. Connotations are the feelings or attitudes associated with a word or phrase—associations beyond the literal meaning of the term. Consider these word pairs:

retreat	strategic withdrawal
intellectual	egghead
sweat	perspire
drunk	inebriated
boyish prank	vandalism
collateral damage	civilian casualties
psychiatrist	shrink
downsized	fired
revenue enhancements	tax increases
guerrillas	freedom fighters

The words in each pair refer to the same object or state of affairs, but the images or emotions conveyed are dramatically disparate.

To write well, you must be aware of both the literal meaning of words and their connotations. You must also understand that people often use connotations to put an argument or view in a negative or positive light, one that may be misleading or partisan. In debates about abortion, for example, those who oppose abortion may refer to their position as "pro-life" or "pro-child." Those opposed to this view may call it "anti-choice" or even "anti-woman." In disputes about gun ownership, those who want to restrict gun ownership may label their position "anti-assault weapon." Those opposed to this position may call it "anti-self defense." Such labels are intended to provoke particular attitudes toward the subject matter—attitudes that may not be justified by any evidence or argument.

Words used to convey positive or neutral attitudes or emotions in place of more negative ones are known as euphemisms (for example, *neutralize* for *kill*). Words used to convey negative attitudes or emotions in place of neutral or positive ones are called dysphemisms (*dive* for *tavern*). Both euphemisms and dysphemisms can be used to mislead. As a critical reader, you should be on guard against the deceptive use of connotations. As a critical writer, you should rely primarily on argument and evidence to make your case.

Remember, however, that euphemisms often serve legitimate purposes by allowing people to discuss sensitive subjects in an unobjectionable way. You may spare a person's feelings by saying that his or her loved one "has passed" or "passed on" rather than "has died" or that his or her dog "was put to sleep" rather than "killed."

Rule 8-6   Learn to Distinguish Words That Writers Frequently Mix Up

adverse: contrary to, opposed to
averse: disinclined, being ill-disposed to

affect: *v.* to influence
effect: *v.* to accomplish; *n.* result

allusion: indirect or veiled reference
illusion: faulty perception, delusion

beside: near
besides: apart from, also

compliment: *n.* praise; *v.* to praise
complement: *n.* counterpart, supplement; *v.* to complete or supplement

comprise: to include, to consist of (e.g., The whole *comprises* the parts.)

compose: to make up (e.g., The parts *compose* the whole.)

continuous: occurring uninterrupted, unceasing
continual: frequently recurring, occurring intermittently

disinterested: impartial
uninterested: not interested

enormity: extreme evil or wickedness
enormousness: bigness

ensure: make sure, guarantee
insure: buy or give financial insurance

farther: at a greater *physical* distance
further: at a greater figurative distance (e.g., We discussed the issue further.)

flout: to express contempt for
flaunt: to show off

fortuitous: *adj.* happening by chance
fortunate: *adj.* lucky

imminent: *adj.* happening soon, impending
eminent: *adj.* notable, distinguished

infer: to deduce
imply: to suggest

lay: *v.* to place (e.g., Lay the book down.)
lie: *v.* to recline; past tense is *lay* (e.g., I will *lie* on the couch, and I *lay* on the couch yesterday.)

like: *prep.* similar to [a noun or noun phrase] (e.g., She looks like Karen.)

as: *conj.* similar to [verbs or clauses] (e.g., She looks as if she ran a mile.)

literally: actually, in the literal sense of the word, without figurative language

figuratively: metaphorically, in the figurative sense

oral: spoken

verbal: having to do with words

principal: *adj.* chief, main; *n.* head of a school

principle: *n.* basic truth, law, doctrine

Rule 8-7   Strive for Freshness; Avoid Clichés

A cliché is an overused, stale expression, the kind you should try to avoid in all your writing. Clichés were once fresh and interesting ways of expressing an idea. Overuse, however, drained the life out of them. *Blind as a bat, busy as a bee, playing with fire, light as a feather, saved by the bell, water over the dam*—these and many other trite expressions show up in student writing frequently. They signal to readers that the writer is not putting much original thought into the composition. Even worse, they prevent writers from thinking for themselves and achieving a novel perspective.

Clichés, of course, can sometimes help you say something accurately. You should, however, avoid them when you can and develop the habit of reaching for originality.

Here are some clichés that you may be tempted to use:

birds of a feather	thick as thieves
bolt from the blue	diamond in the rough
lock, stock, and barrel	burning the midnight oil
nutty as a fruitcake	avoid like the plague
cool as a cucumber	fly in the ointment
red as a beet	raining cats and dogs
beat around the bush	water under the bridge
mountains out of molehills	bull in a china shop
nip it in the bud	comparing apples and oranges
pull no punches	hook, line, and sinker

Rule 8-8   Do Not Mix Metaphors

Metaphors can be extremely effective in compositions. Using metaphorical language effectively, however, is not easy, and you should not attempt it unless you are confident of the results. Most of the time, using no metaphors is better than concocting metaphors that are poorly made or confused.

A problem common in student papers is the mixed metaphor—a mixture of images that do not fit well together. Alone, each image may convey a coherent idea, but together the images form a ludicrous, even impossible, picture.

MIXED: In this administration, the ship of state has thrown in the towel on affirmative action and marched to the beat of a different drummer.

The clash of these incongruent images—the ship of state, throwing in the towel, and marching to a drumbeat—is distracting, confusing, and laughable. If there ever was a serious point here, the mixed metaphor killed it. (In addition to the images being mixed, they are clichés.)

Here is another one:

MIXED: Because it is pointless to try to teach an old dog new tricks, we decided to throw all our efforts into low gear.

An image derived from dog training is coupled with one from vehicular gear-shifting. The picture conjured up is strange and unenlightening.

The best way to avoid mixed metaphors (and most other miscues with metaphorical language) is to try to visualize the image you create. If your visualization reveals a coherent, apt picture, then your metaphor may be acceptable. If your picture is defective, revision or deletion is in order.

Rule 8-9   Beware of Awkward Repetition

When handled carefully, the repetition of words can achieve emphasis, cohesion, and emotive force. Clumsy repetition, however, offends the ear and signals an inexperienced hand.

CAREFUL REPETITION: Next to the enormous war and the massive landscape and the huge sky, she seemed ever so small, with small hands clutching her small child, living in a small village in a small shack, which held a small bag containing everything she had.

AWKWARD REPETITION: We are studying so we might understand more about Spinoza and understand his main ideas.

AWKWARD REPETITION: The tendency to write repetitiously is a tendency that can only be corrected through practice.

AWKWARD REPETITION: As soon as you do the analysis on the projections, you can check the analysis against the files.

AWKWARD REPETITION: He could see that two ducks were on the pond, three ducks were on the dock, and five ducks were missing.

⊰ Appendix A ⊱

Formatting Your Paper

The formatting conventions discussed here are used in the humanities and are consistent with the general guidelines in *The Chicago Manual of Style*. The formatting preferences of your instructor, of course, trump anything in this appendix.

GENERAL SPECIFICATIONS

- Use good-quality paper (neither onion-skin thickness nor card stock), 8½ × 11, white.
- Use a 12-point standard font such as Times New Roman, a common word-processing font. Select a comparable font if you use a typewriter instead of a computer.
- Ensure that there are margins of at least one inch at the top, bottom, and sides of the page. Double-space the text.
- Assign consecutive numbers to all pages, starting with 1, and insert the numbers in the upper right corner of each page. The first page is the title page. Do not show the page number on the title page (see page 127). The first visible page number should begin on the next page—page 2 (see page 128).
- On the title page, center (1) the full title of your essay, (2) your name, (3) the title of the course, (4) your instructor's name, and (5) the date.

Utilitarianism and Our Considered Moral Judgments

Alice Swanson

Philosophy 233: Introduction to Ethics

Professor Smith

15 October 2004

2

Many people believe that God is a lawgiver who alone defines what actions are right and wrong. God, in other words, is the author of morality; an action is right if and only if God commands it to be done. According to this view, there is no right or wrong until God says so, and nothing is moral or immoral independently of God's willing it to be thus. God, and only God, *makes* rightness and wrongness. This view is known as the divine command theory of morality.

A simple version of the theory is widely accepted today, among both the religious and nonreligious. In this version, God is thought to be the source of all moral principles and values. He can be the source of all morality because he is omnipotent, being able to do anything whatsoever, including create the very foundations of right and wrong.

In the *Euthyphro*, Socrates brings out what is probably the oldest and strongest criticism of the theory. He asks, in effect, is an action right because God commands it to be done, or does God command it to be done because it is right? This question lays bare the dilemma that is inherent in the theory: If an action is right because God commands it, then there is nothing in the action itself that makes it right, and God's command is arbitrary. If God commands the action because it is right (that is, he does not *make* it right), then rightness would seem to be independent of (or prior to) God, and the divine command theory is false. I contend that, at least in the simplest version of the theory, this ancient dilemma still stands and that the most plausible way to resolve it is to reject the theory by accepting that moral standards must exist independently of God's commands.

The central argument against the notion that rightness is whatever God commands is this: If an action is right only because God commands it (that is, nothing is right or

QUOTATIONS AND CITATIONS

- Block quotes are usually separated from regular text by leaving a blank line before and after the block quote and by indenting the left edge of the block quote four or five spaces. For an example, see page 130.

- Start endnotes on their own page. Number the endnote pages along with the rest of the pages. Center *Notes* at the top of the page. Indent endnotes as shown on page 131.

- Single-space each endnote. Insert one line space between entries.

- Start a list of works cited on its own page. Number the pages with the rest of the paper. Center *Works Cited* at the top of the page. Indent entries as shown on page 132.

- Double-space each line of works cited notes.

- Use a notes page as a model for the spacing in a bibliography. Start a bibliography on its own page; number the pages along with the rest of the paper. Indent a bibliography as you would a works cited page (Rule 6-4).

5

If a prediction turns out to be false, we can always save the hypothesis by
modifying the background theory. As Philip Kitcher notes:

> Individual scientific claims do not, and cannot, confront the evidence one
> by one. Rather . . . "hypotheses are tested in bundles." . . . We can only
> test relatively large bundles of claims. What this means is that when our
> experiments go awry we are not logically compelled to select any
> particular claim as the culprit. We can always save a cherished hypothesis
> from refutation by rejecting (however implausibly) one of the other
> members of the bundle. Of course, this is exactly what I did in the
> illustration of Newton and the apple above. Faced with disappointing
> results, I suggested that we could abandon the (tacit) additional claim that
> no large forces besides gravity were operating on the apple....Creationists
> can appeal to naïve falsificationism to show that evolution is not a science.
> But, given the traditional picture of theory and evidence I have sketched,
> one can appeal to naïve falsificationism to show that *any* science is not a
> science.[4]

To see this point, let's examine Christopher Columbus's claim that the Earth
is round. Both Christopher Columbus and Nicholas Copernicus rejected the flat
Earth hypothesis on the grounds that its predictions were contrary to experience.

7

Notes

1. Alasdair MacIntyre, *A Short History of Ethics* (New York: Macmillan, 1966), 178-79.

2. Brooke Noel Moore and Kenneth Bruder, *Philosophy: The Power of Ideas* (Mountain View, Calif.: Mayfield, 1990), 285.

3. Joel Fineberg, ed., *Reason and Responsibility* (Belmont, Calif.: Wadsworth, 1981), 430.

4. MacIntyre, 190.

5. Moore and Bruder, 411.

6. John Scott, review of Limits of Imagination, by Samantha Speers, *American Journal of Imaginative Studies* 10 (1990): 321-34.

7. Peter Suber, *Guide to Philosophy on the Internet*, April 1999, <http://www.earlham.edu/~peters/philinks.htm> (7 May 2005).

8. Saul Traiger, "Hume on Finding an Impression of the Self," *Hume Studies* 11, no. 1 (April 1985), <http://www.humesociety.org/hs/issues/v11n1/traiger/traiger-v11n1.pdf> (1 October 2004).

9. Norman Melchert, "Nature Philosophers," in *The Great Conversation* (Mountain View, Calif.: Mayfield, 1991), 7-15.

10. MacIntyre, 234.

11. Traiger.

12. John R. Searle, "Minds, Brains, and Programs," *Behavioral and Brain Sciences* 3 (1980): 417-424.

Works Cited

Johnson, Larry. *The Ancient Greeks*. New York: Putnam-Bantam, 1979.

---. *The Hellenic Age*. New York: Oxford-Putnam, 1999.

Jones, Nathaniel, and Katharine Wendell, eds. *Philosophy and Religion*. Mountain View:

Greenland, 1956.

MacIntyre, Alasdair. *After Virtue*. Indianapolis: Notre Dame, 1984. 1 October 2004

<http://www.luc.edu/depts/philosophy/tec/eac6/macintyre-tradition.pdf>.

Simpson, Carol. *Time's Arrow: The Ancient Conceptions of Time, Motion, and Symmetry*.

Mountain View: Upton, 1980.

Smith, Nancy H., et al. *Philosophy, Mathematics, and Mysticism in Ancient Times*. 5th

ed. Mountain View: Greenland, 1967.

Suber, Peter. *Guide to Philosophy on the Internet*. Apr. 1999. 1 October 2004

<http://www.earlham.edu/~peters/philinks.htm>.

Traiger, Saul. "Hume on Finding an Impression of the Self." *Hume Studies* 11.1 (April

1985): 22 pars. 1 Oct. 2004 <http://www.humesociety.org/hs/issues/v11n1/

traiger/traiger-v11n1.pdf>.

⊰ APPENDIX B ⊱

Documenting Your Sources

THE CMS DOCUMENTARY-NOTE SYSTEM

In this approach, note numbers are inserted into the text in superscript, in consecutive order, after all punctuation marks (but not the dash), and at the end of the relevant text passage. (See the note numbers in the quoted passages throughout this book.) Each note number, of course, refers to a corresponding reference note, which may be treated as a footnote or endnote. If the notes are treated as footnotes, they are placed in numerical order at the bottom of the page on which the corresponding note numbers appear. If they are treated as endnotes, they are gathered together in a numerical-order list at the end of the paper under the heading "Notes." (See the sample page of endnotes on page 131.)

Reference notes must contain all relevant publication information so that readers can easily find sources for review or study. To ensure that the information is accessible and useful to readers, the notes must consistently follow a specified format, which varies depending what kind of source is being cited. The first time a source is cited in a note, the note must include a full citation—that is, all the required information (author's name, title of publication, city and year of publication, publisher, etc.) in the proper order. All later reference notes for the same source should be abbreviated and, in the case of books, may consist of just the author's last name and a page number. (For example: Johnson, 99.) Later notes referring to multiple works by the same author should also be abbreviated but include a condensed version of the work's title.

(For example: Johnson, *Greeks and Ancient*, 153 [refers to a book]; or Johnson, "Ideas Rising," 340 [refers to an article].)

The following sections illustrate the proper CMS note format for the first, full reference of several different types of sources. Notice that the usual sequence of information for a simple note is: name of author or authors; title of the book (or article plus journal name); city of publication; name of publisher; year of publication; page numbers.

BOOKS

To find a book's publication information, look at the title page first then the copyright page. See note 1 below for an example of how subsequent references to the same book are shortened.

One, two, or three authors

1. Alasdair MacIntyre, *A Short History of Ethics* (New York: Macmillan, 1966), 178–79.

[Note: Book title always italicized or underlined.]

Subsequent reference to same book

33. MacIntyre, 165.

Subsequent reference to another book by same author includes abbreviated title

47. MacIntyre, *After Virtue*, 104.

2. Brooke Noel Moore and Kenneth Bruder, *Philosophy: The Power of Ideas* (Mountain View, Calif.: Mayfield, 1990), 285.

3. Stanley M. Honer, Thomas C. Hunt, and Dennis L. Okholm, *Invitation to Philosophy* (Belmont, Calif.: Wadsworth, 1992), 49–52.

More than three authors

4. Greg Bassham et al., *Critical Thinking: A Student's Introduction* (Boston: McGraw-Hill, 2002), 155.

Editor, translator, or compiler but no author

5. Joel Feineberg, ed., *Reason and Responsibility* (Belmont, Calif.: Wadsworth, 1981), 430.

6. Gerald Forbes and Nina Johnson, trans., *Prose from the North Country* (Dayton, Ohio: Ingram and Consetti, 1989), 342.

7. Gregory Knopf, comp. *Complete Papers of Nonia Forge* (London: Hutton Kind, 1949), 347.

Editor, translator, or compiler with an author

8. Edgar Eddington, *Edge of Night*, ed. Maureen Dodd (Buffalo: Tiffton Press, 1966), 213.

[Note: Author's name first; editor, translator, compiler name after title.]

No author

9. *Bound for Glory* (Eugene: Winston-Hane, 1976), 343.

Later editions

10. Irving M. Copi and Carl Cohen, *Introduction to Logic*, 9th ed. (New York: Macmillan, 1994), 109.

Chapter in a book

11. Norman Melchert, "Nature Philosophers," in *The Great Conversation* (New York: Oxford University Press, 2007), 7–15.

Essay in an anthology

12. Theodore Thomas, "Reason and the Abortion Debate," in *The Debates of Our Times*, ed. Dorothy Silvers (New York: Warrington Press, 1966), 45.

Preface, foreword, or introduction

13. John Smith, introduction to *Reason and Rhetoric*, by Theodore Thomas (New York: Warrington Press, 1966), 89.

[Note: Author of introduction mentioned first; author of book itself follows title.]

Specific volume in a multivolume set

14. Thomas Kane, *The Issues of the 21st Century*, vol. 5 of *The Issues of History* (New York: Warrington Press, 1955), 222.

[Note: Citation refers to whole volume.]

15. Thomas Kane, *The Issues of History* (New York: Warrington Press, 1955), 4:125–40.

[Note: This format is used when the volume title is not given. Citation refers to volume 4 and page numbers 125–40.]

Entire multivolume set

16. Mary Ingram, ed., *International Law and Commerce*, 4 vols. (London: Greenland Press, 1951).

Corporate author

17. National Literature Council, *Literature in the Classroom* (New York: National Literature Council, 2001).

PERIODICALS

See note 18 for an example of how subsequent references to the same article are abbreviated.

Journal article

18. John R. Searle, "Minds, Brains, and Programs," *Behavioral and Brain Sciences* 3 (1980): 417–24.

[Note: Citation indicates volume 3, publication date of 1980, and pages 417–24. Article titles are always enclosed in quotation marks; journal names, in italics or underlined. For journals whose page numbers run consecutively from the beginning of the year to the end through all issues (that is, all pages are in the same volume), the volume number, page numbers, and year are sufficient for identification, as in the example here. For journals whose page numbers start at page 1 in each issue, both volume number and issue number must be cited. For example: *Behavioral and Brain Sciences* 3, no. 4 (1980): 417–24. The volume number is 3; the issue number, 4.]

Subsequent reference to same article:

32. Searle, 420.

Subsequent reference to another article by same author includes abbreviated article title:

40. Searle, "Is the Brain's Mind," 420.

19. Edmund L. Gettier, "Is Justified True Belief Knowledge?" *Analysis* 23 (1963): 121–23.

[Note: No comma is required after the article title when the title ends in a question mark or exclamation point.]

Magazine article

20. Patrick Huyghe, "Moody's Crystal Ball," *Omni*, June 1989, 90.

[Note: Includes month and year in date without an intervening comma.]

21. Seymour M. Hersh, "Annals of National Security: The Iran Game," *New Yorker*, 3 December 2001, 42–50.

[Note: Day of the month precedes the month without intervening punctuation.]

Book review

22. John Scott, review of *Limits of Imagination*, by Samantha Speers, *American Journal of Imaginative Studies* 10 (1990): 321–34.

[Note: Author of review is mentioned first; author of book, stated after book title.]

23. Nicholas Lemann, "Pure Act," review of *Theodore Rex*, by Edmund Morris, *New Yorker*, 19 November 2001, 81–84.

Newspaper article

24. David Jackson, "The Rise in Crime," *Buffalo Eagle-News*, 3 November 2003, late edition.

[Note: Page numbers are not included.]

25. Editorial, *Buffalo Eagle-News*, 3 November 2003, late edition.

26. "Edward Jones, Dead at 86," *Buffalo Eagle-News*, 3 November 2003, late edition.

[Note: No author mentioned.]

ONLINE WORKS

The CMS does not contain guidelines for citing Internet sources. A documentation system based on CMS principles, however, has been devised for Internet citations. It has been worked out in *Online! A Reference Guide to Using Internet Sources* (Boston: Bedford/St. Martin's, 2000) by Andrew Harnack and Eugene Kleppinger (see <http://www.bedfordstmartins.com/online/index.html>). The following sample notes conform to these recommendations. (Remember, subsequent references to the same source are abbreviated, just as they are for books and periodicals.)

Whole website

27. Peter Suber, *Guide to Philosophy on the Internet*, April 1999, <http://www.earlham.edu/~peters/philinks.htm> (7 May 2005). [Note: Site title is italicized. First date is date of publication; second is date site was accessed.]

Online book

28. Alasdair MacIntyre, "The Nature of the Virtues," in *After Virtue*, March 2000, <http://www.netlibrary.com/EbookDetails. aspx> (1 October 2004).

[Note: If publication information for the print version of the book is known, it should be included in place of the online publication date. For example: Alasdair MacIntyre, "The Nature of the Virtues," in After Virtue (Notre Dame: University of Notre Dame Press, 1984), <http://www.netlibrary.com/EbookDetails.aspx> (1 October 2004).]

Journal article (ejournal)

29. Saul Traiger, "Hume on Finding an Impression of the Self," *Hume Studies* 11, no. 1 (April 1985), <http://departments. oxy.edu/philosophy/hs/issues/v11n1/traiger/traiger-v11n1.pdf> (1 October 2004).

[Note: If the website has no page numbers, substitute document divisions such as Preface or Conclusion.]

Magazine article

30. Naomi Klein, "You Can't Bomb Beliefs," *Nation*, 19 October 2004, <http://www.thenation.com/doc.mhtml?i=20041018 &s=klein> (1 November 2004).

THE MLA AUTHOR-PAGE SYSTEM

In this approach to documentation, the source is typically indicated in the text by the author's last name (either in a phrase or in parentheses) and the relevant page number (in parentheses). The in-text citation refers the reader to a list of works cited where more detailed information is given about the source. The list is alphabetized according to the authors' last names, with exceptions for sources without authors.

In-Text Citations

In a typical citation, if the author is mentioned in the text, only the page number is required in parentheses.

According to MacIntyre, Montesquieu seems to have believed in unshakeable ethical norms while also embracing a kind of ethical relativism (178).

If the author is not mentioned in the text, however, both the author's last name and the relevant page number are enclosed in parentheses.

Montesquieu seems to have believed in unshakeable ethical norms while also embracing a kind of ethical relativism (MacIntyre 178).

Notice that the parenthetical information appears at the end of the relevant passage. There is no comma between the author's name and the page number, and the parentheses are inserted in front of the period.

Here are some examples illustrating variations on the typical in-text citation.

Two or three authors

Moore and Bruder discuss early skepticism and comment on Protagoras (128–29).

Early skepticism and Protagoras are inextricably linked (Moore and Bruder 128–29).

The anthology, however, never did justice to Kant's work, especially the writings of the later period (Bender, Smith, and Atwood 308).

More than three authors

Secondary education still seems to deemphasize critical thinking skills (Jones et al. 144–45).

More than one work by the same author

The quality of secondary education seems to vary considerably throughout the world (Jones, "Schools" 435).
[Note: Author not mentioned in text. Material in parentheses gives author's last name, abbreviated title, and page number. Quotation marks indicate title of short work such as an article or short stories.]

Jones argues that the quality of secondary education varies considerably throughout the world ("Schools" 435).
[Note: Author mentioned in text.]

Phillip Jones argues in *Schools of Tomorrow* that the quality of secondary education varies considerably throughout the world (435).
[Note: Both author and title in text.]

Entire work

In *Critical Thinking*, Larry Wright focuses on analytical reading.
[Note: Parentheses and page numbers unnecessary.]

Considerable work has already been done to make analytical reading a main focus of critical thinking (Wright).
[Note: Wright is author of only one work and is not named in sentence.]

Unknown author

Some philosophical arguments have never completely retired from the public square ("Philosophical" 92).
[Note: "Philosophical" is abbreviated title of short work; work is alphabetized in works cited by abbreviated title.]

Part of a multivolume set

The last two hundred years of that period saw very little progress in philosophy and mathematics (Michaels 5: 689).
[Note: Indicates volume 5 and page 689.]

According to Michaels, the last two hundred years of that period were unimpressive (5: 689).
[Note: Author is mentioned in text.]

Entire volume of a multivolume set

In the Hellenic period, philosophy seemed to flounder (Henry, vol. 3).

Authors (of different works) with the same last name

George Smith offered a powerful argument against federalism (650).

In 1801, a powerful argument was offered against federalism (G. Smith 650).

Corporate author

Double-blind controlled trials have shown that large doses of the vitamin are ineffective against cancer (Natl. Cancer Institute 77).
[Note: In parentheses, name of corporate author is abbreviated if possible.]

According to the National Cancer Institute, double-blind controlled trials have shown that large doses of the vitamin are ineffective against cancer (77).
[Note: In text, name of corporate author is spelled out in full.]

Essay or excerpt in an anthology

In "The Dilemma of Determinism," William James argues that indeterminism makes free action possible (333).
[Note: Page number refers to page in anthology.]

In science and everyday affairs, the notions of determinism and indeterminism are in conflict (James 333).

Indirect quotation

Russell says "no priest or churchman will attend me at my deathbed" (qtd. in Jones 56).
[Note: Here "qtd. in" (quoted in) is used to signal that the quotation comes not directly from the speaker quoted but from someone else quoting the original speaker or writer.]

Two or more sources

> The ancient Greeks, however, were a strange mix of rationalism, mysticism, and paganism (Frederick 22; Hoffman 456).
> [Note: Two sources in parentheses separated by a semicolon.]

Works Cited

The list of works cited is meant to be a complete record of all the sources used in the writing of a paper. Readers should be able to look at the list and glean enough information to access every source mentioned. The list has a standardized format, with the sources laid out in alphabetical order by author's last name or, if the author is unknown, by the first word of the source's title. Titles of books and periodicals are italicized or underlined. (See the sample page of works cited on page 132.)

The MLA style helps ensure that the authors' names will be readable and easy to find. The first line of an entry is set flush left, but remaining lines are indented.

Here are some examples of entries for several types of sources.

BOOKS

One author

> Simpson, Carol. *Time's Arrow: The Ancient Conceptions of Time, Motion, and Symmetry.* Mountain View: Upton, 1980.

More than one work by the same author

> Johnson, Larry. *The Ancient Greeks.* New York: Putnam-Bantam, 1979.
>
> ---. *The Hellenic Age.* New York: Oxford-Putnam, 1999.
>
> ---. *The Wars of Alexander.* New York: Putnam-Bantam, 1990.
>
> [Note: Three hyphens plus a period in place of name.]

Two or three authors

> Smith, Nancy H., and John Morgan. *Great Philosophy in the Ancient World.* Mountain View: Greenland, 1990.
>
> Smith, Nancy H., John Morgan, and J. C. England. *Great Philosophy in Plato's Time.* 4th ed. Mountain View: Greenland, 1966.

More than three authors

Smith, Nancy H., et al. *Philosophy, Mathematics, and Mysticism in Ancient Times*. 5th ed. Mountain View: Greenland, 1967.

Corporate author

National Philosophical Fund. *Employment Prospects for Philosophers*. New York: Huffman, 1970.

Essay or excerpt in an anthology

Keen, Janice. "Utilitarianism Revisited." *Readings in Moral Philosophy*. Ed. Gregory Stillman. New York: Huffman, 1922. 300–12.

Collection of essays

Jones, Nathaniel, and Katharine Wendell, eds. *Philosophy and Religion*. Mountain View: Greenland, 1956.

Later editions

Simpson, Carol. *Time's Arrow: The Ancient Conceptions of Time, Motion, and Symmetry*. 4th ed. Mountain View: Upton, 1940.

Entry in a reference work

"Ethical Naturalism." *Oxford Dictionary of Philosophy*. 1996.

PERIODICALS

Journal article

Jones, Nathaniel. "Empiricism Revisited." *Philosophy and Religion*. 6 (1994): 28–35.
[Note: Citation indicates volume 6, publication date of 1994, and pages 28–35. Article titles are always enclosed in quotation marks; journal names, in italics or underlined. For journals whose page numbers run consecutively from the beginning of the year to the end through all issues (that is, all pages are in the same volume), the volume number, year, and page numbers are sufficient for identification, as in this example. For journals whose page numbers start at page 1 in each issue, both volume number and issue number must be cited. For example: *Philosophy and Religion*. 6.2 (1994): 28–35. The volume number is 6; the issue number, 2. The two numbers are separated by a period.]

Magazine article

> Davis, Samantha. "Ethics in the Workplace." *Harper's* Jan. 1991: 60–63.
> [Note: Article title is enclosed in quotation marks; name of magazine is italicized or underlined. Volume and issue number should not be included.]

Book review

> Jensen, Eileen. "When Politics and Philosophy Meet." Rev. of *Commander-in-Chief*, by Jonathan Sosa. *Harper's* Jan. 2001: 56–62.
> [Note: Name of reviewer appears first; author of book appears after book title.]

Newspaper article

> Jackson, Edward. "Abortion Protests Continue." *New York Times* 4 Oct. 2004, national ed.: A21.
> [Note: Article title is enclosed in quotation marks; name of newspaper is italicized or underlined. Volume and issue number should not be included.]

ONLINE WORKS

For additional help in including online sources in a works cited list, see the MLA *Handbook for Writers of Research Papers* (6th ed., 2003).

Whole website

> Suber, Peter. *Guide to Philosophy on the Internet*. Apr. 1999. 1 October 2004 <http://www.earlham.edu/~peters/philinks.htm>
> [Note: Site title is italicized or underlined. First date is date of online publication or latest update; second is date site was accessed. If author's name is unknown, use the site title.]

Online book

> MacIntyre, Alasdair. *After Virtue*. Indianapolis: Notre Dame, 1984. 1 October 2004 <http://www.netlibrary.com/EbookDetails.aspx>.
> [Note: "Indianapolis: Notre Dame, 1984" is the book's print publication information. Date before website address is date of access.]

Journal article (ejournal)

Traiger, Saul. "Hume on Finding an Impression of the Self." *Hume Studies* 11.1 (April 1985): 22 pars. 1 Oct. 2004 <http://departments.oxy.edu/philosophy/hs/issues/v11n1/traiger/traiger-v11n1.pdf>.

[Note: After the title, the information is volume and issue numbers (11.1), date of publication or last update, number of paragraphs in the document, the date of access, and the website address.]

Magazine article

Klein, Naomi. "You Can't Bomb Beliefs." *Nation* 19 Oct. 2004. 1 Nov. 2004 <http://www.thenation.com/doc.mhtml?i=20041018&s=klein>.

⊰ Index ⊱